FOR PARENTS ONLY:

TIPS FOR SURVIVING THE JOURNEY FROM HOMEROOM TO DORM ROOM

Julia Johnston
and
Mary Kay Shanley

Illustrations by Tom Kerr

BARRON'S

All inquiries should be addressed to:
Barron's Educational Series, Inc.
250 Wireless Boulevard
Hauppauge, New York 11788
http://www.barronseduc.com

International Standard Book No. 0-7641-1311-9

Library of Congress Catalog Card No. 99-59073

Library of Congress Cataloging-in-Publication Data

Johnston, Julia, 1943—
    For parents only: tips for surviving the journey from homeroom to dorm room/Julia Johnston and Mary Kay Shanley.
        p. cm.
    Includes index.
    ISBN 0-7641-1311-9 (alk. paper)
    1. Education, Higher—Parent participation—United States. 2. College choice—United States. 3. Universities and colleges—United States—Admission. I. Shanley, Mary Kay. II. Title.

LB2350.5 .J65 2000
378.1'61—dc21

                                                            99-59073

Printed in the United States of America
9 8 7 6 5 4 3 2 1

Contents

Chapter 9
SENIORITIS — IS IT CURABLE?   163

Chapter 10
LEAVING HOME — SLOWLY, IT SUDDENLY HAPPENS   183

INTRODUCTION:

WHY DID WE WRITE THIS BOOK ANYWAY?

We wrote the book you're reading now for a very simple reason: There's a lot our parents never told us—including how to coach our children to get into college. We plunged in, relying on counselors, admissions officers, neighbors, reams of printed material, guesswork, good luck, and blind faith. Here's what we and more than 100 other parents discovered, so you don't have to depend on your parents to tell you.

IF ONLY WE HAD KNOWN THEN...

Once upon a time, there were two families who lived in the same neighborhood. In each family, there was a dad who worked in an office, a stay-at-home mom who baked cookies and wrote for a living, and three little children. The children played in sandboxes and watched "Sesame Street." They did story hour at the library and took swimming lessons. And sometimes they ate the cookie dough before it even got to the oven.

As you'd expect, the children grew. Within a few years, all of them had gone off to elementary school where they learned about numbers and words. Basketballs replaced sandboxes, and hoops were really high up on the garage. Next came middle school where the numbers were in algebra books and the circle of friends changed hourly. Then came high school where they realized that they were becoming young adults with minds and lives of their own. And that was just for starters.

All of this caused the moms and dads to exclaim, "Wow! What happened here? Our kids are growing up so fast! They'll be going to college in just a few short years. Maybe we should start planning for that."

The moms and dads spent most of their waking hours trying to figure their kids out, discovering how to help them prepare for college and considering every method short of bank robbery to pay for tuition, room and board, and books. The parents accomplished all of this despite the fact that their kids didn't think they had the brains of an ant and refused to be seen with them in public.

Now the children are young adults. They've earned diplomas, are on their own, and have decided that their parents are smarter but don't know why. The dads still work in their offices and the moms still write for a living. (They even bake cookies on occasion.) One day, the moms said, "Wow! Getting those kids through high school and into college was quite an experience. We learned a lot from that. Maybe we should write about it so other families will know what to expect. Readers can identify with what we say because we've been there, done that." And that is how this book came to be.

For Parents Only: Tips for Surviving the Journey from Homeroom to Dorm Room covers the expected and the unexpected. It contains a healthy dose of humor—which is more important than aspirin in the college-planning process. And it is based on the real-life experiences of parents of not-always-predictable kids.

PARENTS FROM AROUND THE COUNTRY WHO HAVE "BEEN THERE, DONE THAT"

We realized early on that the way *we* got through the college-planning process may not be the *only* way. So we decided to seek input from other parents who also put their children through college and—obviously—lived to talk about it.

NIGHTS AT THE ROUNDTABLE

We set up roundtables in cities and towns across the United States, each consisting of up to ten parents who were married, divorced, widowed, rich, not-so-rich, and ethnically diverse. One parent's philosophy may have been opposite another's; yet all statements were accepted by the group as having value. We have included apparently conflicting advice in this book for the same reason: It all has value and you must determine its usefulness for your situation.

Before each roundtable, we provided parents with a list of discussion topics, figuring people would talk for two hours, then go home. Instead, people spent three-plus hours at each roundtable. Most arrived as strangers to one another and to us. All of us left as friends, connected inextricably by time spent sharing thoughts, some of which we'd never articulated before.

We'd like to tell you a bit about the parents we met:

- They have a refreshing sense of love and respect for their offspring. They discussed children lost in the wilderness, struggling and confused. They talked about growing pains—theirs and their kids'. But they never, *ever* used the words "bad" or "failure."

- They laughed a lot, declaring that you simply can't get through this part of life without a sense of humor. (Of course, some of the experiences sounded much funnier in the roundtable than they had seemed at the time.)

- They provided their children with the mental, spiritual, and emotional space to grow. They did not try to orchestrate, opting instead to accept that the child's personality and moral background would serve as the guiding force. They taught their children to make choices and allowed the kids—and themselves—to live with the consequences.

- They did not believe it was the teacher's or counselor's responsibility to make sure their student succeeded. Rather, they viewed success as the joint responsibility of parent, child, and school.

- They shared some of the most difficult moments in the lives of their families. One couple shared that after their daughter was offered an outstanding academic scholarship, they decided not to voice their concerns about the college. After the daughter had a miserable freshman year, the parents didn't make that mistake again. An African-American mother spoke eloquently to a room of white parents about the need for her children to attend colleges where they were no longer a minority. She believed it would enhance their self-worth to be in a community of achievers with the same color skin. The list could go on and on. What emerged was a sense of respect for each parent's feelings of inadequacy balanced against his or her desire to obtain what's best for the child.

- They felt hesitant to give advice, but were anxious to share stories about what happened in their families. From these stories, we extracted advice.

- And they believed with all their hearts that learning and education were of paramount importance to their children's self-sufficiency and long-term happiness.

The people with whom we shared time were parents with and without college degrees, but they all had expertise from real-life experience. We as writers are richer for having met them. You and your child will be richer for what they had to say.

CHAPTER 1

HIGH SCHOOLERS: KEEP THOSE KIDS TAKING MATH AND SCIENCE AND LOOKING FOR FROGS

Just when your teenager won't be seen in public with you, it's time for talks that end in decisions that make a difference for college options. Here are tips on how to nurture an early interest in college. Also included is advice about high school classes and activities—stuff your kids think you don't know anything about.

GETTING READY TO GET READY FOR COLLEGE

VOICES OF EXPERIENCE

"In third grade, for whatever reason we didn't know, our son said he wanted to go to college at the University of Rhode Island. Just for fun, I called the university's Admissions Office and bookstore, respectively, and got them to send an application and a sweatshirt for him. He wore that sweatshirt everywhere."

Joe Kirsch

"The difference between my son and me—my dad didn't graduate from high school. I was never expected to go to college. In fact, I didn't decide to go until after my senior year. With our son, there was no other expectation than he would go to college."

Orlo Shroyer

"Our son was set on going to the United States Air Force Academy from an early age. So when he was a freshman in high school, he talked to a recruiter at a college fair. Afterward, he said it was a good thing he went to that fair. 'No way I'm marching into dinner,' he announced. Then, he started looking at other colleges."

Janet Heimbuch

Getting ready to get ready for college is tough. For starters, in the beginning parents are the only ones getting ready to get ready.

The zits have come out, the kids think they know everything, and college is not on the list of topics most freshmen and sophomores think about.

Face it. You can shout from the rooftop about planning for the future, but for your student, the future is this weekend. Kids this age don't believe they'll need to think about college for at least a million years.

Be vigilant! Students who've always been academically sound can lose their way in high school. Little wonder! Hormones have kicked in; it's not cool to be smart; boys need to be muscular; girls need to be thin, and *everybody* needs to be in the "popular" group. (Hence, an excellent reason for you to take long walks alone.)

In fact, by now most girls have often pretty much gone underground academically. Unless you maintain that vigilance, constantly pointing out opportunities, it could be paradise lost by the time they crawl back out of the hole.

Be equally vigilant with your boys. Boys aim to be bulky before brainy, so they won't be nicknamed "Toothpick" forever after.

In case the word doesn't make it home, the message from high school counselors to kids is three-fold:

1. Pay attention to your grade point average (GPA). Although it's always important, colleges pay more attention to later GPAs. (A weak freshman/strong junior or senior GPA is better than vice versa because it shows improvement.) With some colleges, the junior GPA will be the final one that figures into the admissions deadline. Other colleges keep track of you through second semester, senior year. Best advice? Keep studying!
2. Get help with class selection.
3. Know college entrance requirements for your state schools.

Do not let well-meaning friends and relatives ask your child, "So, whatdayawannabe when you grow up?" Most kids don't have a clue. Or today they want to teach and tomorrow they want to walk on Mars. That's why career exploration is so important.

Actually, kids' likes and dislikes already point the way toward some college options. For example, your student likes frogs, hates dancing. Regard that as a clue. Encourage her to take four years of science and math, and sign her up for ecology camp instead of ballet.

VOICES OF EXPERIENCE

"When I was growing up, I realized the worst thing I could have done to my parents was to say I wasn't going to college. Our kids grew up in that same environment."

Jane Eckstein

"I went to the informational talk, where the counselors discussed which classes to take depending upon what your youngster wanted to do—college, technical school, the armed forces or immediate entry into a job. I didn't really need to go to the meeting because the counselor already knew which classes my child needed. Still, my child knew I went and that was important."

Susan Cole

NEVER SAY, "YOU *HAVE* TO GO TO COLLEGE."

VOICES OF EXPERIENCE

"My oldest son didn't want to go to college. He had no idea what he wanted to be. But I forced him to go, and I insisted that he try out for the swim team as he'd been a swimmer in high school. By the middle of his sophomore year, he said he was burned out. He quit swimming, quit college, and joined the Marines. Now, 13 years later, he's a drill instructor and teaches swimming and water survival. He is taking college courses at the same time to finish his degree because he wants to."

Jim Evans

"We never talked about anything but Grade 16 from an early age, so there was always the expectation they would go to college."

Susan Cole

"I was a laborer and took pride in my work, but I had calluses and dirty hands when I came home. I did horrendous 36-hour shifts. One day, Rose brought the kids to see me. I was 60 feet up in a building under construction and afraid of heights. I came down and the kids said, 'Why are you up there?' I said, 'To feed you. If you get a good education, you won't have to work so hard.' "

Rich Kelly

You can say certain things to a kid this age. Things like, "You have to eat pizza," or "You have to stay up late and watch garbage on TV," or "You have to talk for hours on the phone." But never say, "You have to go to college." The results just won't be the same.

Instead, assume your child is college-bound and let the youngster know it. Say things like, "I know you don't agree, *but* when you're in college, you'll miss my telling you to eat your vegetables." That attitude gives direction and definition to the choices to be made. Gently steering your child toward the going-to-college mode will more likely produce the results you're after.

- Nurturing counts. And osmosis is a wonderful thing. Mix with people (and their kids) who show they value education and learning. It might just rub off on your child, too.

- Parent ingenuity counts, too. Let's say you're discussing college with another adult and your teenager is in the other room. Slip into a whisper—then teenagers always think you're saying something they shouldn't know, and they'll listen to every word.

- Encourage your youngster to hang out with smart kids who like to learn, confident kids who have their heads screwed on straight, and students whose values fit your own. Peer pressure can do what parents can't.

- It's time for you to hang out at the bookstores and bring home some college-planning books. You can read them, but your youngster may treat them as though they're a communicable disease. Leave them around anyway.

- Also, encourage your child to bring home printouts of college information he's found on computers at school. Sometimes students have to use the college finder and career finder software in classes, or they may have access during study halls or before and after school.

- Go to initial meetings about high school class choices and college presented by school counselors and parent groups, even if you've already launched an older child into college. First, it shows that you value this youngster's future. Second, you may learn something new.

- Go to area college fairs with your youngster, usually in the fall. Pick up college brochures and financial aid information—and stop by for ice cream on the way home.

- Visit college campuses as part of summer trips after ninth and tenth grades. But be casual—just soak up the aura quickly on your way to somewhere else. Your youngster probably isn't into details right now.

- Drop by large, small, urban, suburban, rural, famous, not-so-famous, majority, and historically black institutions. It's a good way for youngsters to get the feel of different types of campuses. Your child may realize she loves concrete more than trees as you visit urban and rural schools.

- If there is an older sibling or friend living on campus, send the high schooler off for a weekend visit. Your kids may actually get along when you aren't around! Still, don't count on the visit to create in your high schooler's young heart this burning desire to be in college. Be ready for surprises, too. One youngster came home from visiting big brother and reported that he got to collect the quarters during the beer slide.

- Take kids to free or low-cost local college events: street painting for a special weekend; notorious speakers with controversial, current topics; a sporting event; or a stage play.

- Colleges also offer special interest camps during the summer—computers, foreign language, drama, writing, science, math, debate—and on and on and on. Kids glom onto the in-depth, hands-on learning and thrive on mixing with peers who want to learn, too. Also, that's the first snip-snip of the umbilical cord for when kids leave for college.

- If you want your kid to end up at a college in the Rockies, send her to summer basketball camps at colleges in Colorado or Montana. If you want your youngster to attend a large school, send him to summer basketball camps at Big Ten schools. If you want your youngster to go to a small, rural college…well, you get the idea.

- Finally, encourage your high schooler to make a simple list of all the colleges that have flitted through her mind and put them in a three-tiered list: **a)** I want to go there! **b)** Okay, I'll go there, and **c)** If I have to (pout, pout), I will. Remind her that she won't be married to the list for better or for worse.

VOICES OF EXPERIENCE

"We used to include college visits as part of our vacation trip whenever one of our kids was in that summer between ninth and tenth grades. The schools we were visiting had parent sessions, so we would go to them and take the tour."

Jane Eckstein

"One night when our son was a sophomore, we brought home a bunch of college books. We left some in his room and some downstairs. At first, he wasn't real happy about that. He'd pass them in a room and moan. Gradually, we saw him begin to read the books and never heard another complaint."

Ronni Kirsch

"You can sense if your child should go to college or not. Our daughter always wanted to go to college. Our son had a bad experience in grade school and never wanted to go to college. He went to work in the family business and is doing fine."

Jacquie Evans

COLLECTIONS, HOBBIES, AND FOLLOWING DIFFERENT DRUMMERS

VOICES OF EXPERIENCE

"Our son's hobby was to be involved in any way possible with the creek that ran behind our house. He built BMX bike trails and jumps, caught crawdads—anything. He still maintains those interests. Now he's going to take me fly-fishing because he's concerned that I don't have any hobbies."

John Heskett

"When my daughter was small, she would bring home frogs, worms, and all kinds of things to show me. I'd look at the critters and listen to her; then I'd go into my room and cry because I was so afraid of them. And I tried not to overreact when I found them in my bed!"

Eunice Harris

Happy the parent whose kid has hobbies. They teach a youngster how to make choices, pick friends, and socialize.

If your child loudly proclaims an intense dislike for anything unique, listen, smile, and encourage open-mindedness. You never know what creativity may be unearthed by your patience.

- Breathe a sigh of relief when your child's latest passion is for something other than the opposite sex. Then talk about that passion, whether it's astronomy or art. Discuss how the subject translates into making a living. (Kids like real-world connections.)

- Realize that passions pass at this age. If your youngster says, "All I'm ever going to do when I grow up is write poetry that doesn't rhyme," don't take it literally.

- Value your child's differentness. Encourage her to follow that different drummer and to hang out with other independent kids whose happiness barometers aren't pressured by popularity. (This is one of those sounds-simple/is-difficult situations.)

- Let neither rain, wind, sleet, nor snow keep you from delivering your support, whether your child's efforts be in fine-tuning the game of croquet or belting out the blues on a harmonica.

- Know the difference, however, between "support" and "push." Parents tend to place tremendous pressure on youngsters to excel at this age.

But the fact is that most kids know where they fit, and they'll get there more quickly with parental encouragement than with relentless pushing.

The weeding out process has started by now. If the first hobby your student tosses out is the one you most wanted him to keep, remember who's doing the tossing. (Hey, if you liked the hobby that well, maybe you should take it up yourself.)

"Our son wants to do everything. He has two guitars and a drum. Now he's a one-man band. I tell him, 'You can't do everything,' but he is a very impulsive person. He puts pressure on himself and that is just the way it is."

Jennifer Merlin

THE "I-WANT-TO-BE-WITH-MY-FRIENDS" CLASSES—CORE SUBJECTS AND ELECTIVES

"Our son's high school college counselor sent a letter to all the parents of the ninth graders in our son's school. His message was that now, everything counts. It all goes on the high school transcript so students need to start paying attention. The kids talked a lot about that letter among themselves."

Ronni Kirsch

"My daughter perceived that she was viewed by others as a smart nerd. In reality, that may not have been the case but it shaped her actions as she tried to become 'cool.' She actually had plenty of dates in high school, but the perception was that she did not because of being a smart nerd."

Maricel York

It's a bummer! Once your youngster gets to high school, he won't see his friends as often during the day. That's why some kids think signing up for classes with their friends is a good idea. It isn't—and even if they did take the same subject classes, they might be in different sections. That would be another bummer!

A message to the parent: Colleges look at your child's ninth grade work.

Parent's response: "I know that."

A message to the ninth grader: Colleges look at your ninth grade work.

Ninth grader's response: "They don't either."

(Good luck!)

> **Rule #1. Make friends with a good high school guidance counselor today! (Sometimes, that won't be the counselor to whom your child is assigned.)**

> **Rule #2: If you sense the assigned counselor is not effective for meeting your child's needs, it's okay to request a change to another counselor.**

Ask the counselor which classes will be most helpful to your college-bound student. Then, become an advocate for those classes.

Be sure your youngster takes enough math, science, foreign language, and writing courses to meet college entrance requirements. Having four years of literature courses under the belt may not be enough to meet everybody's standards.

TAKE THE CHALLENGE

The prospect of taking challenging courses can lead to all manner of conversations. Like this:

Youngster: "But if I take those classes, I'll have to study every night! They're hard."

Parent: "Try them and see how much time they really take. If you don't have any free time, we'll look at making some changes."

Youngster: "But my best friend is taking easier classes and we want to be together."

Parent: "Each of you has to do what's best for you. Eat lunch together."

Or like this:

Parent: "My youngster won't make straight A's if she takes those classes you have suggested."

Counselor: "But that's the level your child is ready for. Besides the academic basics, they'll teach her study skills and prepare her for college classes."

Parent: "But she won't feel good about herself if she doesn't get straight As."

Counselor: "Life isn't straight As. When do you expect her to learn that?"

Advanced Placement, or AP, courses are college-level courses offered in high school. Some parents love 'em and some don't.

On the love 'em side:

1. They prepare the student for college work. In fact, high school grades in hard courses are the best predictors of college success. So AP courses are not just to impress the admissions people; they are important to "real time" success.
2. If school is too easy, a student can get lazy and not extend himself. AP courses put the brakes on coasting.
3. AP courses tend to bring out a student's competitive nature, but then, life itself is competitive.

On the don't love 'em side:

1. AP courses are high stress and a lot of work.
2. Students who don't score high enough on the AP exam must take the course again in college.
3. Some colleges and universities won't accept AP coursework in place of their own courses, regardless of how high a student's AP exam score may have been.

Find out which teachers are best about giving lots of feedback on kids' writing. Those teachers can be in any subject area. Make sure your student takes at least one class from at least one of those teachers. She'll hate it because the teacher will make her work on writing, but she'll thank the teacher when she gets to college.

Study the description of classes in the student's handbook. If the "educationese" language baffles you, work with the counselor:

A. Make sure your student is placed at an appropriately challenging level. For example, "basic" or "consumer" math usually is for students who haven't learned the basics and struggle with math.
B. Watch for language indicating courses required for admission to a state university as well as courses that may not be accepted by a state university.
C. Understand the sequences for each subject area. A school may require two writing courses in Language Arts (English) before allowing students to take Advanced Placement (AP) English classes. If your child enters senior year without both writing courses and is denied entrance into the AP class because of it, an "I-didn't-know-about-that rule" response won't help.

D. Although many electives aren't "college prep" classes, they represent an important part of life. Courses such as debate, newspaper, yearbook, art, and music integrate many areas and often involve hands-on learning with products you can read, see, or hear.

E. Encourage your student to take electives outside of the general areas of interest—like 3-D art or a consumer ed course that provides practical information on laundry, cooking, savvy shopping, and etiquette. (You think they're born knowing that stuff?)

LEARN ABOUT THE TEACHERS

Ask other parents about the teachers. Decide which teachers' styles best suit your child's personality and way of learning. Then, encourage your student to request those teachers. The right teacher can make a big difference in academic development.

Get to know each one of your child's teachers. Ask teachers what their expectations are of your youngster and of you. Request that the teachers let you know early on if there are problems. Good parent-teacher relationships are a gift to your child.

If you don't have a home computer, sign your child up for keyboarding during school or for a summer class. College kids take laptops to class, professors have paperless classes with everything communicated via computer, and *e-mail is a part of life today.*

Small, rural schools can't always offer as many class choices as larger schools. Figure out ways to offer learning opportunities beyond the school day: county extension experiences, library usage, computer access to the Internet, family trips, and even old-fashioned board games like Risk, Monopoly, and Clue.

DISTANCE LEARNING

Then there's distance learning, which opens education doors that most parents don't even know exist. With distance learning, your child might:

—take specialized classes your district can't afford to offer by itself;
—enroll in a college class without stepping on the college campus;
—pair up with somebody in another state, another country, or another continent to do a school project or assignment.

Study skills don't always come naturally, even when the person doing the studying has been hanging around books for this many years. Some kids can complete an evening's worth of homework with time left over; others can't even remember to bring the work home. If the latter sounds like your kid, talk to the counselor. If your school doesn't offer a study skills class, suggest the idea to the principal.

Finally, don't underestimate your kid's ability to comprehend the benefits, disadvantages, and consequences of choices and actions. When he wants to talk about those choices, spend more time listening than speaking. (Another one of those sounds-simple/is-difficult things.)

"We had to teach our kids that if they were having trouble in a certain class, and they perceived the teacher was not worth listening to, that person was still the teacher. That is life. You're going to get out in the real world and find that same situation over and over again. You don't sit back, put your feet on the desk, and go to sleep if you think the teacher is dumb."

Mary Beth Lazzaro

ACADEMIC STRESS—A NOT-SO-PRETTY PART OF THOSE "CAREFREE" YEARS

"The kindest thing you can do for children is to help them realize they don't have to be good in everything."

Jacquie Evans

"Our family is just not good in math. When our daughter was a junior, she kept saying, 'I don't know what they are telling me.' So we began looking at alternatives. She had never been in a 'regular' math class before, so it seemed like a step backward. The pressure not to take that step came from her friends, but we were supportive."

Kathy Hafner

"When our son went into ninth grade, he didn't get the same kind of grades that he had been earning and did later. He felt much worse about that than we did. We tried to console him, told him to take things step by step. We asked him why he thought he got a bad grade. Should we go to the back of the chapter to do example problems? Should we go see the teacher? We asked him how [we could help him] to deal with the problem."

Michael Johnston

"Our daughter wanted to take all of these AP classes, but worried about getting Bs. She knew what that would do to her GPA. Her counselor told her to take the AP courses anyway. The counselor said colleges were aware of AP course content, and would rather see students challenge themselves and get Bs than take regular track courses and get A's."

Jim Dakin

Q. How do you know that your child is experiencing academic stress?
A. You live with the kid, don't you?

- Stress comes from the school environment. Some call challenging classes stressful because the student must work hard to achieve just a passing grade; others call "soft" classes stressful because the student becomes so irritated at putting in time and not learning new material.

- Students may feel stressed because they're in regular instead of accelerated or AP classes. They also may feel cheated if they perceive that most of the motivating teachers teach the accelerated classes. Conversely, students may feel stressed because they're in accelerated or AP classes, which demand a truckload of time and work.

- Stress comes from peers. Students believe they need to do as well academically as their friends, which is not always possible.

- Stress comes from parents who push kids beyond where they need to be, or realistically can be. If your student is up studying until three o'clock every morning, ask yourself why.

- Stress comes from society's subtle message: Successful students attend big-name schools. There is an underlying notion that community colleges and most state schools aren't "good enough." But the fact is, they are a very good match for some students.

- Stress comes from within your student. Working to the best of her ability is one thing, but often the message she's getting is that she must achieve beyond her ability—or what she thinks her ability is.

Forever, children have labeled one another. As early as grade school, a child will decide (and often announce) that if somebody isn't in the gifted or accelerated classes, that somebody must be dumb. Or a child will declare that anybody in the accelerated classes is a nerd or geek, neither of which a high school student is proud to be. High school students may not be quite that blunt, but that smart-dumb notion bubbles right below the surface.

It's best if your child makes his own decisions regarding the courses he will take. But the decisions should be based on research, which often begins with the counselor.

You can help your child handle that academic stress simply by being there. Knowing he can count on parent support makes a youngster feel that he isn't out there paddling the canoe all by himself.

Your youngster may not actively seek out your support the way she did when she was younger, but she still needs it. But remember, there's a fine line between supporting and pushing too hard.

Once in a while, however, you may need to slip into the "push" mode, especially when there are opportunities your child could take advantage of but doesn't, either because he isn't paying attention in school or doesn't have the wisdom and experience to see their value. Gentle cajoling and letting the teachers and counselors know that you are always searching for opportunities for your child might help.

Encourage your youngster to network, though he might not call it that. Finding a teacher who especially likes your youngster can do much for perceptions, morale, and stress.

If your youngster is experiencing problems in a particular class, suggest that she meet with the teacher. It's a wonderful habit to cultivate, one that you hope will carry over onto the college campus.

Most kids aren't going to be stellar in every class. There has to be a balance, a time when the student decides how much effort to put into this class and how much into that one.

Reiterate to your youngster that he is a whole person. Academics, as well as extracurricular activities, hobbies, socializing, athletics, and a job all count.

In the end, your child may not be stressed about whether she can get into college, but rather about which college she can get into.

VOICES OF EXPERIENCE

"My daughter took AP American History and she spent so many hours on it that I almost died. Still, you couldn't say to her, 'Get a B,' or 'Get a C.' She had to get an A. By the time she went to college, she already had 36 credits. But did she get through in less than four years? No!"

Dianne Peterson

"The child should be able to look back on those high school years—on memories of friends, football games, and studies, but not memories of harassment or pressure. You don't want your child to say, 'I got a 94 on that exam and Mom thought I should have scored higher so I could maintain that 3.9999 GPA.'"

Vivian Brown

ACTIVITY-ITIS—MAKING AN APPOINTMENT TO SEE YOUR CHILD

"I told our youngest child not to go into band because it meant she would not have time for any other activities she may have been interested in during school. She immediately ignored me and went into band just as her sister and brother before her had done. As soon as we paid for the instrument, it promptly went into the closet with the others."

Eunice Harris

"During our son's junior year, he decided to quit cross-country. We told him he wasn't quitting unless he found a job that took the same amount of time each week. Cross-country or work, one or the other. He'd made a commitment to his team, and we wanted him to understand how important that was. The team needed him for the whole season."

Daniel Lazzaro

Point out connections between what your child likes—music, debate, drama, whatever—and realistic career opportunities. For example, not all musicians go on world tours. Some give trumpet lessons, direct the city's symphony orchestra, or write jingles for toothpaste commercials.

Look for clues as to what your youngster likes and may want to pursue later. Kids this age are notoriously unexcited about anything but they still pick things they like, whether they know it or not. For example, the *I-love-to-shop-but-I-don't-like-to-buy* syndrome might point to a career in research. Suggest activities that might develop those interests and skills.

If you want your child to participate in a variety of activities (and you do), *don't suggest it*. High schoolers don't take kindly to suggestions. Instead, promise you won't take pictures at the vocal music concert. Pretend you don't care whether she signs up for Mock Trial competition. Simply nod your head when your student announces he joined the school newspaper staff.

Brace yourself! You can promise to bake chocolate chip cookies every day for the rest of your life if your youngster will please play basketball *and* flute and your child still may say, "No, thanks." In the end, it may be your desire, but it's your child's life.

Since your child was old enough for water wings classes at the Y, you've been exposing her to a multitude of experiences. Now she's taking over, self-selecting one, two, or three activities to pursue. If they're valid choices, but not ones *you* would have made, it may be time for another one of those long walks alone.

If the problem is being interested in everything, what your youngster may need most is a lesson in time management. Tell her that often, the more highly selective a college is, the more it looks at depth in an activity—what did your child actually do and what were the effects—rather than at breadth.

Continue quietly to identify your youngster's weaknesses, then unobtrusively steer him toward activities that will overcome or compensate for those weaknesses. At the same time, when your child says, "Okay, I've built enough character for now," relax and encourage him to simply enjoy doing what he's good at doing.

VOICES OF EXPERIENCE

"Our daughter was invited to be on a traveling soccer team. This would have involved her being gone on Sundays. We personally didn't feel as though that would be a good idea, but we let her make the decision. She decided her religious training was more important to her than the soccer team. Fortunately, we did not have to intervene, although I think we would have if she had decided the other way."

Jeanie Heskett

COMMUNITY SERVICE—CHORES FOR OTHERS THAT KIDS CAN'T POSSIBLY DO AT HOME

VOICES OF EXPERIENCE

"As a teacher, I'd say that the kids who succeed in academics are more secure in who and what they are. Consequently, they're more ready to branch out and try community service. The debate kids, not the athletes, get involved (in my school). If athletes are involved, they are also academic achievers."

Laurie Crawford

Ignore your youngster's daily declaration that, "As soon as I grow up, I'm moving to a place where there's more stuff to do!" The child really does need and want to be connected to your community. Encourage involvement in community service.

That involvement will come more easily if *you're* active in the community. Kids mimic what they see, which, sometimes, can be a real pain.

The benefits of community service are as diverse as the opportunities. Kids who help in soup kitchens expand their view of the world around them and develop empathy for others. Kids who volunteer to work with younger children in a parks and recreation program develop patience, understanding, and leadership skills. (They also announce at the end of the session that they'll never have kids of their own.)

Community service also exposes kids to career possibilities. For example, if your child is thinking about a career with animals, encourage him to volunteer in an animal shelter.

Community service may give you a leg up in the college search process. Often, selective schools look for depth of commitment to a community service project, believing that it says something special about the student.

Both boys and girls are involved in community service today. There's no gender distinction.

Make sure your child's abilities match the community service project. Is training necessary? Will there be adult supervision and guidance? Will your youngster receive a simple "thank you" at the end of the project? (We sure hope so!)

Help your child understand that her community service may not be saving the world but does make a difference. That in itself is commendable.

Community service opportunities exist in school, through church youth groups, and through one's own initiative. All are equally valuable for personal growth and should be noted on the college application.

Keep a scrapbook or journal of your child's activities and accomplishments, from community service projects to drama awards. Even if the youngster serves a holiday meal for some organization only once, write it down and, if possible, have the child scribble a couple of words about whether the experience was good, bad, or in-between. The payoff? Your youngster will have a great scrapbook and lots of ideas when it comes time to write those college application essays.

"Our daughter taught handicapped children how to ride horses as part of a community service project. She said the experience changed her life."

Rose Kelly

"EVERYBODY ELSE HAS A JOB!"

"Our son worked at a video rental store. He decided that job was at the bottom of the food chain and a college degree was the only way out."

Susie Polden

"Both our kids always went to summer school. That was their job. Then one said he wanted to work during the school year. When? He came home at 6:00 P.M. One time, a pizza place called to offer him a job. They said it would be 30 hours a week. Yeah, right. We didn't even tell him about the call."

Jennifer Merlin

"Our son always had a summer job, but not one during the school year. He wanted to play sports, which I supported."

Michael Johnston

Some high schoolers work to help support the family. Others work to buy a brand new, bright red Jeep Grand Cherokee. There is a difference.

To college admissions representatives, though, jobs (along with activities, community service, and hobbies) are most important to show a student understands the value of work, dependability, and responsibility—characteristics college students definitely need. Kids who are not independent and responsible at the end of high school may or may not survive in college.

Many parents don't want their youngster working during the school year, especially if the child is carrying a heavy academic load or is in extracurricular activities and/or athletics. They believe going to school is a full-time job.

Other parents don't mind their child working during the school year unless the grades begin to suffer. If you sense that is happening, zero in very quickly.

For some kids, work is what gives them pride and self-esteem. When they graduate, they can say, "I've already had three jobs!"

Minimum-wage jobs make higher education look appealing, no matter how tough the coursework. After spending weekends or summer months greeting people at the front of a drug superstore or saying, "May I help you?" at a fast-food drive-in, there may be nothing they won't want to accomplish academically.

HOW MANY HOURS?

For most kids, working 12 to 15 hours a week is plenty. For almost all kids, 20 hours a week during the school year is too much. Still, some students end up working 30 hours a week, closing the store, and falling asleep in class the next day. That's true in part because when an employer asks hardworking students to do more, most won't say no for fear of losing their jobs.

Your student may be the most responsible person in the place and shouldn't hesitate to say, "Enough is enough," when asked to do more than he should. Who's going to fire a responsible, thinking part-timer?

For most kids, it's easier to find a summer job they don't want to do than to find a summer job they do want to do.

The youngster who earns minimum wage at a summer job also learns responsibility.

Some parents don't require their child to work if the youngster spends a certain number of hours each week as a volunteer.

A job during senior year can help curb senioritis (see Chapter 9) because the youngster has to be responsible to someone else besides you, someone who's paying him, too.

Your student needs to understand that just because she receives a paycheck doesn't mean the money is all hers to keep. For example, you may provide a car for your high schooler to drive, but insist that she make the insurance payments. And if sharing a paycheck with the insurance company doesn't shock the kid into the real world, sharing even more of that paycheck with Uncle Sam will.

Sometimes, jobs can help a youngster with career options better than an aptitude test or interest survey. (In fact, with or without jobs, have your child take school aptitude tests or interest surveys during junior and senior years. A pattern may emerge to give even a tiny bit of direction.)

Jobs should be like stepping-stones, with one building from another. Understanding the process may help your child sense his own direction or passion developing.

VOICES OF EXPERIENCE

"Our daughter clerked in a store and had a lot of responsibility throughout high school. By the time she was a senior, we noted that a lot of the kids were sort of checking out before school was over. Because of her experience in the world of work, quitting as a senior didn't fit."

Bud Bennett

"We nixed the idea of our kids working even though they didn't have many of the same luxury goods as their friends. Our philosophy was the kids were going to spend most of a paycheck on consumer goods they didn't need to be happy. Their real job was school, which included challenging classes and activities. That amounted to days that put them in school at 6:00 A.M. and home at 7:00 P.M. or later, and then homework in the evenings—more than a full-time job equivalent. They were learning all the social and leadership skills. And, they were too busy and tired to ever cause any problems or need a curfew."

Jim Adams

MENTORS—YOU'D BE SURPRISED WHO THEY ARE!

VOICES OF EXPERIENCE

"My dad was in the printing business. He encouraged a small boy who came by to take all the extra paper Dad had left around for drawing. Dad praised his drawings, even though my dad didn't know anything about art. The boy grew up and did some music and art design for one of [singer/songwriter] Kris Kristofferson's albums. A mentor can be somebody you just come across in your life, not necessarily a teacher."

Susan Cole

Mentors aren't always teachers by profession, but they do a whale of a job of teaching about the world of work. If your youngster works, a mentor could be the boss, who shows by example.

Encourage your child to follow a mentor around for a morning or afternoon. (Just hope the mentor isn't having a bad day! Of course, *that* may be a lesson in itself.)

Youngsters connected with mentors can learn by osmosis what they didn't know enough to ask about at the career fair.

Sometimes, mentors don't have a thing to do with career choices. Rather, they are friendly listeners whom your child respects, and who respect your child. Count yourself lucky. After all, high school students view most parental suggestions as ridiculous, to put it kindly. But those same suggestions coming from other adults sound great!

Sometimes, volunteer mentors are part of either a school- or community-sponsored program. Your guidance counselor should be aware of such programs. The mentors may put on formal presentations about college preparation, or simply provide advice on an informal basis.

Other very good mentors have no connection with a formal program. Maybe the mentor is a classmate's parent. Kids will often tell a friend's parent stuff they'd never tell you! Which is okay. You probably don't want to know everything anyway!

Maybe the mentor is a neighbor who writes well and will look over your child's college application essays.

Maybe the mentor is a co-worker who does lots of interviewing and will help your youngster prepare for campus visits.

And maybe, just maybe, your child will seek out these mentors herself. Kids have an uncanny knack for sizing up adults. Ferreting out and using such resources is the sign of a together young person. And that in itself will serve your child well in college.

VOICES OF EXPERIENCE

"Talking to everybody—welders, college grads—is so helpful. Kids begin to realize that whatever they do, they probably won't do it forever. We want them to say, 'Okay, while I'm here, I'm going to give this job everything I have and I'm going to learn everything I can.' "

Kathy Hafner

STILL TEACHING INDEPENDENCE AND RESPONSIBILITY

Can we talk? It's like this: Kids who aren't fairly independent and responsible by the time they graduate from high school usually have very short college careers.

You probably started fostering these qualities when your child was crawling around, munching on dirt. Even so, we know the kid is still a work-in-progress. And because high school brings on so many other challenges and changes, we have a few suggestions that may help that work-in-progress progress:

1. Break down a big chore into several smaller ones. Want a perfect example? What about the youngster who is so overwhelmed by the fact that there are a million colleges to choose from that he can't figure out where to start, much less which campuses he should visit later on? You could suggest he read this book, since that's what it is all about. However, he won't (which is why you are). So, pass on the advice our parents are offering you:

   - Suggest your child create a list of parameters—points that he wants or doesn't want in a particular college.
   - Have him gather information about colleges that fall into those parameters. There are sources from the counselor's office to the bookstore to the Internet to the neighbor's youngster.
   - Once he has some idea of the college possibilities, talk about money. (Trust us—that is a valid process of elimination!)
   - Finally, he'll know enough to begin compiling a very real list of colleges to consider. And he'll be so darned proud of himself!

2. With your youngster, set three small goals to be met each day. During the school year, insist two of the goals pertain to academic projects.

3. When crunch time rolls around (and it will, no matter how organized your youngster might be), have the child make a daily to-do list. If the first item is "Make a list," the kid can cross that one off as soon as the list is complete. It makes a person feel darned good!

4. Buy your child a planner or a large calendar in which she will be expected to write down doctor's appointments, library due dates, soccer practices, art classes, or whatever. While you should appear to

rely on your child to remember these dates, the fact of the matter is, you'd better copy the dates down yourself. Then, if your youngster appears to have forgotten about the haircut appointment next Tuesday at 4:00 P.M., you can say, "Didn't you say you have an appointment for a trim one of these days?" It's a very clever approach and almost always works.

5. Each evening before bed, help your child get in the habit of looking at the planner to see what's on the agenda for tomorrow. Let your youngster pile stuff by the door at night to grab on the way out in the morning.

6. Here's the hard part: Don't rescue your youngster. No more taking the forgotten sneakers, homework, or lab materials to school. If he has to take detention, so be it. It probably will help your student figure out how to do a better job of remembering.

READREADREADREADREAD

If you've been encouraging reading all these years, you deserve a medal. If you haven't been, it is never too late to start. Either way, one of your jobs is to get that youngster's nose in a good book. Reading is so vital to your child's future that any way, any time you can encourage it, you must. It's part of good parenting.

The best time to begin reading is when the child is still so young that all he or she does is burp, soil diapers, and cry. The reading thing progresses in a fairly predictable pattern: First, the little one sits on the parent's lap, slapping away at the book. Then, the little one sits on the parent's lap, knowing exactly when the parent should turn the page in a favorite story. Eventually, the little one sits beside the parent, "reading" in a creative manner, followed by the youngster sitting beside the parent, reading a new book to the parent. Finally, the child sits alone, reading to himself or herself.

Hey, where did the parent go? Many parents (and researchers) think the parent and child should have continued reading, both to each other and quietly to themselves. A parent seen reading shows how important reading actually is. And like it or not, children do what children see.

One of the ways you can help prepare your child for college is to continue encouraging reading in many forms, *even when the youngster is bigger than you are*. May we suggest:

- **READ THE SAME BOOK AT THE SAME TIME, DISCUSSING IT AS YOU GO.** (This makes for great dinner conversation.) Your perspectives will be different and your horizons will be broadened because youngsters say the most surprising things.

- **DISSECT THE BOOK YOU READ TOGETHER.** What was the author trying to accomplish? How did the author bring you into the story? How did you "know" the main characters? How did the author make you laugh or cry? Or was the book a bomb? If one of you liked it and the other did not, so much the richer for conversation.

- **READ A BOOK THAT HAS BEEN MADE INTO A MOVIE.** Afterward, rent the movie; then discuss how the movie differs from the book. Most likely, whole portions of the book or specific characters will not appear in the production. Who agreed with the decisions and why?

- **TURN OFF THE TELEVISION FOR 30 MINUTES EACH EVENING.** Use the time for free reading, as opposed to assigned reading. That goes for you as well as your child. If you don't believe there is time to do this, reexamine your priorities.

- **OR SAY, "NO TV," NO MATTER WHAT TIME YOUR YOUNG-STER GETS HOME FROM SCHOOL.** Have a snack, newspapers, and magazines handy; don't ask a lot of questions immediately, and give your child time to unwind—reading.

- **ENCOURAGE YOUR CHILD TO READ THE NEWSPAPER EVERY DAY.** Discuss different sections and what the purpose of each might be. Both of you follow a current event in the newspaper. Watch the evening news together, and compare how the event is handled on TV and in the newspaper. That helps both of you become more savvy consumers of news.

- **REWARD GRADE REPORTS WITH A BOOK PURCHASE.** Half-price or used bookstores are treasures…more books for less money. Give or make a bookshelf or bookcase as a special present.

- **PLANNING A FAMILY VACATION?** Ask each family member to research one of the destinations. Then, have a group confab to discuss all the possibilities for family fun before everybody piles into the car.

- **READ A STORY.** First, you read to your youngster, but promise not to tell anybody outside of the immediate family. (Maybe, sometimes, it will be a story you wrote.) Then listen when your youngster wants to read a story to you. (Maybe sometimes, it will be a story your child wrote.)

THAT GENDER INEQUITY THING—BAD FOR GIRLS, BAD FOR BOYS

A young man studying for his doctorate in physics at one of America's most prestigious schools is one in a class of 17—15 males, 2 females. The young man uses empirical data to draw a conclusion about the gender ratio: Fewer women are interested in, and fewer women do science than men.

That gender difference wasn't always that way. Research shows that girls start out ahead of boys in speaking, reading, and counting. In the early grades, their academic performance is equal to boys in math and science. But as the girls get older, those test scores, nationally, tend to decline. The boys' scores, however, continue to rise and, eventually, surpass the girls', especially in math and science.

When our young man was in middle school, his girl classmates didn't do as well as he and some of his male friends did in math and science. By high school, the ratio of male-to-female in classes such as AP physics, AP chemistry, and calculus was lopsided. And, typically, the few girls in those classes said little.

That gender ratio widened in college to such an extent that by the time he arrived at graduate school, he took the 15-2 split for granted.

Gender inequity, of course, goes far beyond girls' test scores in math and science. It is damaging to *both* sexes. (Boys tend to skip out of foreign language earlier, or avoid it altogether; that eliminates some colleges from their list of potential choices.) Basically, gender inequity short-circuits everybody and, in the end, nobody wins. So whether your child is a male or female, you need to be aware of the issue. In the teen years, it manifests itself in girls with not only a decline in math and science scores, but also a lack of willingness to take those classes. They also demonstrate a loss of self-esteem. The manifestation in boys is not as obvious, but the damage can be just as great.

So, what's a parent to do?

- Learn more about gender inequity. That's a must whether you have a son or daughter or both. Understanding a problem is the first step toward dealing with it.

- Be more proactive than your parents were in expanding your daughter's and son's horizons and understanding.

- Encourage your son to be a caretaker. Look for men in his life who can demonstrate that attribute.

- Encourage your daughter to be a risk taker. Look for women in her life who can demonstrate that attribute.

- Investigate the stereotypes perpetuated within your own family. Monitor your words and actions. Do you call your son(s) and daughter(s) "guys" when you'd never call a mixed group "gals"?

- Don't wrinkle your nose and say, "Eee-ooo" when your son sketches clothing designs or your daughter waxes poetic about dissecting frogs in biology.

- Tell stories to your children with the theme that they can be anything they want. Well, wait. Your daughter may have trouble playing third base for the Boston Red Sox, but she could work in management for the team or play for the professional Women's National Basketball Association. And your son may have trouble—uhm, uh, whoops, we can't think of a single good example to give you here. Well, guess he couldn't join the WNBA!

- Try some role reversals at home. Mom grills; dad does the dishes; brother dusts; sister mows.

- If you have children of both sexes, make sure your girl gets to talk (and is heard) as much as your boy. Likewise, help your son develop good listening skills, which often come more naturally to girls.

- Encourage your daughter to hang out with other girls who are achievers. Support and encourage relationships with boys as well.

- Discuss the conflicting messages your children receive from TV, peers, society, and school. Point them in the direction of strong women and men role models. Introduce them to your friends and acquaintances and describe their work.

- Discuss issues of gender equity with your children. It's vital that boys and girls understand the equal worth both males and females bring to the school and community. Your message still may fail to penetrate, but keep trying.

- Read the same books your children are reading. If the message is not one of gender equity, discuss it.

- Talk regularly with your daughter's teachers about class participation. Don't assume you'll be called when problems first arise. Usually, the call comes after problems have had plenty of opportunity to fester.

- Listen to your children's questions, worries, and comments about school and their peers. Read between the lines. Children often ask for help without actually asking for help.

- Ask teachers, counselors, and other parents about opportunities for girls and boys through Saturday and summer programs at colleges. Expand horizons through workshops and activities that highlight nontraditional areas such as math and science for girls and writing and foreign language for boys.

- Set the same high standards in academics, activities, and career exploration for your daughter and your son.

- Be aware that daughters are more inclined to attend to their homework than are sons. Make a point of knowing your son's homework responsibilities and monitor completion.

- Remind your daughter to speak out; remind your son to delve and reveal a bit about himself.

AND THE WINNER IS...

Sports, sports, sports. Encouraging sports participation and high fives is one thing. But it's a whole 'nother thing to lead children to see sports as *the* most worthwhile activity and to view themselves as queen or king of the gym, and often, consequently, of the home. Finding the balance keys later decisions about activities and college options. Here's what parents say about the wide world of sports:

- **TAKE A REALITY CHECK.** Do you want your child to stay on a team because you never got the chance to play? Does playing on the team mean your kid can't be a kid anymore?

- **TRY TO KEEP ATHLETICS IN PERSPECTIVE.** Very few youngsters grow up to earn a living as an athlete (and support us in the style to which we'd like to become accustomed!).

- **SIZE OF SCHOOL MATTERS WITH SPORTS.** Kids in larger school districts face tough competition for coveted spots on high school teams, while kids in rural areas get to participate in just about every sport offered. Consider the differences if you have a choice about where your child goes to school.

- **SPORTS CAN BE CRUEL TO CHILDREN WHO PHYSICALLY DEVELOP LATER.** For example, your high school child may learn how to deal with "pine time" in basketball, even with a no-cut rule. That's because no-cut doesn't mean every person gets playing time. It's heartbreaking to see your kid's hopes for stardom dismissed so quickly, but the great thing is that kids survive very well. Here's where other activities really help.

- **HIGH FIVES COUNT IN INDIVIDUAL SPORTS SUCH AS COMPETITIVE SWIMMING OR TENNIS.** Like football or basketball, individual sports also teach goal setting, discipline, and concentration.

- **THINK OF SPORTS AS A LEARNING LABORATORY FOR SOCIAL GROWTH.** Just as in real life, there will be both happy and unhappy times.

CHAPTER 2

PREAPPLICATION PROCESS— ORGANIZATION BEATS CHAOS EVERY TIME

Finding college information is like looking for a big pitchfork in a little haystack. But finding the *right* college gets back to the needle-in-the-haystack thing. Here are tips for organizing the search, what's important and what you can ignore, plus some shortcuts that save time and maybe even a few bucks.

AVOIDING THE DART BOARD SYNDROME—BEGINNING AND NARROWING THE COLLEGE SEARCH

"Watch for early signs of separation anxiety. When our daughter was little, she wouldn't even go away to camp. We told her she had to go either to camp or to her grandparents' house. So she went to her grandparents but she took a friend along. The summer before she was a junior in high school, she traveled to Germany and was extremely upset at being away from her family. We were advised that she shouldn't go to a college more than two hours away from home, and she didn't. Even then, we still had to deal with the whole issue of separation."

Karen Dakin

"The first thing one of my kids looked up in each new brochure we received was the male-female ratio on campus. If it wasn't what the youngster wanted, the brochure went into the trash right away."

Jim Adams

"My daughter simply wouldn't apply to any college that required an essay."

Lee Galles

"Our son watched a couple of college videos and decided they were just promo jobs. He was right. He wanted something more objective. Another video was a turnoff for him because it showed a campus full of kids on skateboards, and he didn't want to go to a school where everybody was a jock."

Susie Polden

In the beginning, rule out nothing. Even students who are absolutely, positively, without a doubt set on a particular school may have second thoughts when given the opportunity to compare it with other colleges.

Although promoting college as a general goal in ninth and tenth grades provides a strong base, starting the search process in earnest before junior year could create major burnout. (That's when your youngster cuts you off in mid-sentence with a loud "Fergeddaboudit! That's all you ever talk about!")

During your youngster's first year or two of high school, don't pressure him so much about choosing colleges that making a choice becomes a chore rather than a rite of passage.

Still, realize now that:

1. Choosing a college requires a lot of time;
2. Time is a rare commodity for juniors and seniors;
3. If you haven't at least begun the search by your child's junior year, get going! You can still make something happen; you'll just have to pedal faster.

Even then, you may have to cajole your junior more than you'd think. Many juniors are not ready to accept actually doing the college search, though they might claim they're mature enough for a 2:00 A.M. curfew on school nights.

Now hear this!! If kids are interested in the U.S. service academies such as West Point, Annapolis, or the Air Force Academy, senior year usually is too late to start. High school juniors need to file precandidate forms with the academies. The process and timing are different from regular colleges. (See "Yes, Sir! I Want to Go to a Service Academy, Sir!" on page 50.)

SOURCES

For nonservice schools, look at the ratings of colleges and programs in various publications, but don't rely on them as the sole determinant. Different publications use different criteria and weighting to arrive at a rating. And as one parent kept telling her kids, "Ratings aren't everything!"

Don't underestimate the value of parent networking to find out everything and then some about colleges near and far. Of course, some of what you hear may be more fiction than fact. That happens when stories get passed around and around.

Some closer-to-the-truth sources are as near as your public library and the guidance office. Check out objective books for factual information such as size and tuition. Then read the books that talk about subjective things such as whether sports reign supreme outside the classroom.

Read the college catalogs. Sounds simple, doesn't it? But many parents and students ignore those boring books with the small print. Catalogs describe every course and which semesters each course is given, the class attendance policy, what specific courses are required for a major, how low the grade point goes before suspension, how to appeal grades—just about everything your student will ever need to know except what time to go to bed.

These days, some people say they find more information from the web site than in those glossy brochures.

Some schools have videos you can borrow. The parents will watch videos by the hour, but the kid is always too busy. (Maybe you should give the video an R rating and see what happens!)

MATCHING NEEDS

Your child must consider schools that will meet her needs, but bear in mind that schools also must consider students who will meet their needs.

Schools generally look favorably upon matches between what your student wants and what the institution offers. Say your child declares, "Music is my life!"—and then applies to schools where most music comes from a boom box. Or your child states categorically, "I have to study forests or I'll, like, die!"—and then applies to schools with no forestry program. This will cause admissions officers to scratch their heads and discard the application.

CREATING THE LIST

Now comes the tough part, where you suggest that your child begin to create The Long, Meandering List of Colleges (see Appendices). Your suggestion may be met with one of two responses:

A. "Yeah, okay. I'll get right on that." (It's a start.)
B. "Only a parent would come up with an idea like that!" (Persist anyway.)

Buy an accordion folder, or maybe a bunch of accordion folders, and suggest that your child assign a different slot to each college that makes its way onto The Long, Meandering List of Colleges. Right now, neither of you has a clue about the blizzard of information that soon will be inside your home.

We know, we know . . . your youngster should take on much of the responsibility for all of this. Even so, you'll need to double-check with the guidance office periodically for important deadlines, newsletters, dates of visits to the high school by college representatives, and scholarship information. This is one more part of parenting nobody told you about 16 or so years ago.

What if you're the only one pushing college? The truth is, not every youngster is ready to go to college directly out of high school. And the harder you push, the more your child is likely to say, "No college for me, no matter what!" That answer might come from that contrary gene teens nurture so well, but still, you need to have a rational discussion—or discussions.

LIFESTYLE CHOICES

Today, teenagers have a tougher time deciding among the smorgasbord of career and lifestyle choices. Some become better college students by working a year and setting goals for why they want to spend the money and study time.

At the same time, living at home like a king or queen for that year doesn't help you or your young adult. Better that your youngster spend the year in "reality time," which includes a full-time job, rent, car insurance, laundry, and the final shocker, no holiday breaks.

Listen closely to see if you can figure out whether your youngster believes college is unthinkable "right now" or "ever in her whole entire life." But don't despair if you can't decide where her head is on this one because she may not know, either.

Enlist the help of the high school counselor for understanding the youngster's motivation and finding other options. Some job and career investigating with your youngster might be fun and yield a clue or two for her.

You still don't give up the idea of college right after high school. After all, when your youngster said, "I'm never going to another basketball game again," you said, "Uh-hmmm," and then watched him go out the door to the game on Friday night.

VOICES OF EXPERIENCE

"By the time we began helping our third child to select a college, she'd already been exposed to a lot of information and had stayed with her older brother and sister on their campuses. So she was good at judging a college according to the information sent to her. She liked personalized letters, not ones sent to her as a Social Security number."

Barbara Walker

"Your child doesn't have to go to the big-name schools to get a good education. Look at schools where you'll feel comfortable."

David Hafner

"Right after Christmas, before the students go back to college, our high school brings in 40 or 50 recent graduates who are now in college. People know them, often because they have younger brothers and sisters still in school. First, they meet with our students, who really like that because they get to ask kid questions. Then, they have a panel discussion for parents."

Nancy Johnson

MY ALMA MATER DOESN'T *HAVE* TO BE YOUR ALMA MATER

"I went to a college of 5,000 and our daughter spent most of her growing up years on that campus. It was like her playground. By the time she went to college, we had moved away from there, but she returned as a student. She knew at least 45 percent of the professors, her self-esteem was high, and she knew no ceiling to her achievements there. There was no stopping her because she chose a comfortable area to live in when she left home."

Jacquie Evans

"Ever since our son was born, we assumed he would go to our alma mater. We took the children with us to campus events and homecoming games. They loved it, but when our son got into high school, he decided he didn't want to go there. The tennis coach at the college—our son's godfather—even offered him a full ride (scholarship). Our son wasn't impressed at all. He knew he wanted to leave the area, to go to a small college, an all-black one where he would have his own identity."

Paula Dawson

Just because everybody in your family for the past three generations went to the same university does not mean your child automatically should go to that university.

Just because everybody in your family went to college in your home state doesn't mean your child was born to stay in-state. Would it be so bad if your youngster crossed over to somebody else's state?

It's okay to nudge a youngster in a particular direction, but she may have a different compass and go places you never imagined. Deep breaths, long walks, you know the drill by now.

Sometimes the only way to get kids to do what you want is to suggest the opposite. Just make sure the opposite is okay in case your kid says, "Great idea!"

"I had taught at the University of Miami and we'd had good experiences there. My son, though, had his sights set on a different school completely. He said, 'It's Your-ami, not My-ami.'"

Gene Eckstein

"My husband and I were Howard University graduates. Since our kids were in majority schools all their lives, we gently steered them toward all-black schools. But since they were influenced by their peers in their high school community, they wanted a majority school—the same schools for which their classmates were competing. They joined black student groups on campus to meet their needs for community."

Joyce Batipps

FIGURING PARAMETERS—A WHOLE LOT OF STUFF TO THINK ABOUT

VOICES OF EXPERIENCE

"From the beginning, I said college was my son's experience and, because of that, I didn't care where he chose to go. But after he picked a school that was ten hours away from home, I felt like, 'Oh no. Don't go that far away!' "

Paula Dawson

"Our son wasn't interested in going Greek. In fact, he excluded one college from his prospective list because the information they sent indicated the campus was 46 percent Greek."

Don Polden

Going to college, whether it's 30, 300, or 3,000 miles from home, is a BIG deal!

Here is a Whole Lot of Stuff to think about and discuss as the college search process begins. Some of these issues will be covered in the college literature; others may need to be addressed during campus visits.

- **SIZE OF SCHOOL.** Schools come in three sizes: big, medium, and small. But early on, don't dismiss an entire category because of size alone. Every size has advantages and disadvantages.

- **GEOGRAPHIC LOCATION.** In what part of the nation is the school located? Is it an urban or rural setting? Will the city mouse be happy in the country? And vice versa?

- **MORE ON GEOGRAPHY.** If a school is relatively selective, it's a good bet that the Admissions Office will want a certain number of students from your area. Such schools seek a student body that reflects every region of the country. The fewer who apply from your area, the better are your child's chances. Even so, a 900 SAT score won't zoom an Alaskan ahead of a 1300 score from New Jersey.

- **EVEN MORE ON GEOGRAPHY.** Some parents encourage their child to go to school in a different part of the country, believing that college then becomes not only an educational opportunity but also a new and broadening life experience.

- **DISTANCE FROM HOME.** If the distance is too great to drive, you probably won't attend a lot of functions that involve parents or ones in which your child is participating. Also, your student probably won't be able to come home more than once or twice during the academic year. Realize, too, that your youngster probably doesn't have much perspective on distance. After all, is there any distance too far to go to hear a favorite rock band?

- **COST.** This is part of the mix for almost everybody. The good news? Cost doesn't automatically rule out private or more costly state schools. Plus, expensive schools have more money to distribute in the form of financial aid than do less expensive schools. The bad news? Expensive schools still make most parents feel as if they are hemorrhaging money for four years.

- **RELIGIOUS AFFILIATION.** Is that important to your family?

- **COED VERSUS SINGLE-GENDER SCHOOLS.** Some kids can't imagine living four years without daily interaction with the opposite sex; others don't care. If your son is girl-crazy, will he feel that something's missing in an all-male school? One student chose a women's college because she didn't want what she called the "distraction" of looking nice all the time; she preferred wearing a coat over her pajamas to breakfast.

- **THE STUDENT BODY.** What's the average age? Do most students live on campus? How about the number of part-time versus full-time students? (Part-time students don't live on campus and often aren't active in campus life. Consequently, colleges with a high percentage of part-timers have a different "feel" than those where most students are full time and on campus.)

- **PEOPLE MIX.** How will your child fit into a school that has mostly people from a particular region or a large percentage of students who went to private prep schools or public schools?

- **ETHNICITY.** What are the percentages of the ethnic student groups on campus? If your child is a member of a small group, talk about whether he would be more comfortable on a campus where he is still a member of a small group. Or would he rather be on a campus where a higher percentage of students share his ethnicity. If your child grew up without experiencing diversity, would a campus with lots of ethnic groups provide a richer college experience?

- **MORE ABOUT ETHNICITY.** Look beyond the student body. What is the ethnic makeup of the faculty and staff? How is ethnicity reflected in the curriculum? What about campus clubs and festivals that celebrate diversity? What about the community in which the college is located?

- **THE SCHOOL'S REPUTATION.** Is it a party school? Are its academics rigorous? (You do not want your student to be bored!) What's the political climate? Liberal? Conservative? Does a degree from that school open doors for graduates?

- **LIVING ARRANGEMENTS.** Do freshmen live together or are they scattered throughout the dormitories? Are there no smoking, no alcohol dorms? Designated quiet floors in some dorms? Do the schools offer a four-year housing guarantee? You think that's not an issue until your youngster calls home and says she's living in the gymnasium!

- **ACADEMICS.** Do the school's academic strengths match your child's areas of interest? Count the number of course offerings in that area and look at the instructors' credentials. Are instructors listed as full-time faculty, part-time staff (adjuncts), or teaching assistants (graduate students)? Are faculty ethnicity and gender balanced? (Check faculty titles and credentials in the catalog.)

- **STUDY ABROAD.** Does the school offer study abroad options that count toward graduation? What percentage of students study abroad? And for one semester or two? Does financial aid apply to study abroad?

- **SERVICE LEARNING.** Learning through helping others can be life-changing experiences for students. What service learning opportunities does the school offer? If service learning is carried out in faraway places, who pays for transportation and housing? Does tuition cover any service learning options? Who sponsors and supervises?

- **GRADUATION RATE.** Is it 98 percent? 89 percent? 75 percent? A lower graduation rate calls for more questions: How many students don't return sophomore year? Are there "weeding out" required classes, which a certain number of students generally fail? Does the academic profile of high school GPA and ACT or SAT scores indicate unprepared students may be regularly admitted?

- **GRADUATE SCHOOL.** Groan. But if your child wants to be an astronaut or doctor or some other profession that requires additional schooling, ask how many of the college's students get into graduate programs and where.

- **CAMPUS SAFETY.** Are there transportation provisions? Good lighting? Is there a commitment to students by administration and by fellow students that helps ensure safety?

- **POLICIES.** Are there written policies and procedures to deal with sexual harassment by students or faculty and staff? How about policies regarding academic conduct, including cheating?

- **THAT WORK THING.** Does the school offer opportunities during the school year and summers to work in the real world doing internships? What are its graduates in your child's field of interest doing now? What percent went on to work where?

Encourage your child to talk with recent high school graduates, especially any who attend colleges that are of interest to your youngster. What those recent graduates have to say will have an impact on your child.

Are you having fun yet? You don't need to obsess about any of these parameters, but you do need to know the answers. Even if your youngster says, "Hey, I don't care about all that stuff!" it's worth it for your peace of mind.

Besides, at this point, your youngster does not understand that the college campus will become her home for the next four or five years. Her happiness quotient will affect her studies.

VOICES OF EXPERIENCE

"Parents assume their son will take care of himself. But they worry about their daughter's physical safety. Why they don't think of doing so with their son I don't know."

Ann Galles

"I told my daughter she couldn't consider schools that were more than 10 hours from home because then I would have to pay for plane tickets."

Sheila Ayala

"We visited the Duke (University) campus and my husband and I were enthralled. It had a fair number of minority students, which suited our daughter fine. We said, 'Don't you love this campus? Don't you just love this school?' She didn't seem very enthused, so finally we asked her what it was that she didn't like. 'I haven't seen any guys with earrings, no one with nose rings or purple hair. What kind of place is this?' she responded. While she's a pretty straight kid who didn't express herself with any particular manner of dress, she respected those kids who did. She enjoys that kind of diversity. Diversity was equally as important as minority representation to her."

Joyce Batipps

CONSULTANTS AND COUNSELORS—
INFORMATION GALORE

VOICES OF EXPERIENCE

"Our high school counselor kept telling our daughter to call if she had questions, and just about held her hand through the early admissions thing. If your child isn't getting support like that from a counselor, you have to ask for a change."

Jim Dakin

"We had a friend who was much involved in her son's college search. The son kept waving her off and finally said, 'You know, Mom, I've been working with this counselor for a couple of years. So should I now work with somebody whose job is to get me into a good college or should I work with my mother?'"

Don Polden

"I knew of someone whose son had had some difficulties in high school. His grades reflected being in a bad peer group. When it became time for college, the college to which he was admitted was not what he preferred. So the family worked with a private counselor who guided him into a program that ultimately would launch him into a better school. They didn't feel like a public school counselor was as networked to do that as was a private counselor."

Diane Lenahan

Independent educational consultants can't get your child into a school, but they probably can help your child get himself into the school.

Consultants identify schools that match your student's interests, personality, academic skills, and budget. They help set up campus visits and offer advice on everything from test taking to filling out the applications to essay writing. Consultants also cost money. But just like paying tuition, some parents look upon this as an investment in their child's future.

Some people think of hiring a private consultant as a safety net. The consultant should know college representatives and network with them.

Not all independent educational consultants are created equal. Check on professional affiliations, years in business, where most of their student clients have gone to school. And talk to the people listed as references. Even so, it doesn't always work out as you hope.

Not all high school counselors are created equal, either. That means you have to watch like a hawk to make sure your youngster is getting the guidance she needs.

In some public schools, counselors are assigned as many as 500 students (or even more!) to oversee. Consequently, the child may need to search out the counselor, rather than wait for the counselor to search out the child. It's that squeaky wheel thing. You've probably experienced it before.

Private high schools with fewer students may offer more college counseling to students. And then again, they may not.

If you don't know what to expect from your counselor, ask parents who were pleased with the help their youngsters received. Then, if your kid is getting rubber-stamped through the system, ask the principal to assign your child to another counselor. We know that doesn't seem like a very polite thing to do, but remember, you are your child's strongest advocate. And your youngster gets only one future.

One wise guidance counselor reassures families by saying: There is a school out there for every one of your kids. We must work to find a match for each special kind of student.

Sad but true: One high achiever in a family may receive more interest and help from counselors and teachers than an average student in the same family. Here's where parents need to do their own research or use outside resources.

Admissions representatives call counselors to ask about parts of a student's record. Counselors also write recommendations for students. So parents need to visit with guidance counselors, too. Then, if your student has a problem, the counselor should have a better handle on the situation and go to bat for the kid.

VOICES OF EXPERIENCE

"We received no direction through the process. I paid $100 for help from a guidance counselor from another school. Still, the information was generic. Then we figured we'd have to find out information for ourselves."

Susie Polden

"While I was sitting in the office, our school counselor called an admissions officer at a college our daughter was interested in. The counselor said, 'I have a woman here with me whose daughter is a bright student but didn't do well on her SATs. What can you do for her?' The admissions officer agreed to accept my daughter, and she wasn't even put on probation. Now our daughter is there on the dean's list."

Dianne Peterson

"YES, SIR! I WANT TO GO TO A SERVICE ACADEMY, SIR!"

Some kids love the military, savor the intense physical and academic competition, or like having a free education. Well, nearly free; the payback is in service time rather than in $$$. Then there are others who believe it's stupid to make your bed when you're just going to crawl between the sheets again that night. In either case, visiting a U.S. academy before deciding it's the place to be is a good idea.

There are five service academies: U.S. Air Force Academy in Colorado Springs, Colorado; U.S. Military Academy in West Point, New York; U.S. Naval Academy in Annapolis, Maryland; U.S. Coast Guard Academy in New London, Connecticut; and, U.S. Merchant Marine in Kings Point, New York. Except for the Coast Guard, which also charges an entrance fee, the academies' application procedures differ from those of civilian colleges. Additionally, students must start the process sooner, which means this option probably isn't for procrastinators.

Here's a general (no pun intended) thumbnail sketch of admissions processes. Do get specifics from each academy.

A. File a precandidate questionnaire with the institution(s) in the spring of the junior year or ASAP after that. (The Coast Guard and Merchant Marine academies do not require precandidate questionnaires.)

B. At the same time, apply for a nomination for admission from members of Congress, other government officials, and/or service departments. (The Coast Guard Academy does not require a nomination.)

C. Take a physical fitness exam and/or a medical exam.

D. Take the ACT and/or SAT.

E. Fill out (and return, of course) other forms after the precandidate questionnaire is okayed. Service academies are part of the government, you know.

Members of Congress often begin examining students' records during the summer before senior year and finish by October. Academies may offer admission as early as November of senior year.

Want more information? Contact:

Air Force Academy, Colorado Springs, Colorado
E-mail: go to web site for on-line form
Web: *www.usafa.edu/rr/*
Phone: 800-443-9266

U.S. Military Academy, West Point, New York
E-mail: *admissions@www.usma.edu*
Web: *www.usma.army.mil/*
Phone: 914-938-4041

U.S. Naval Academy, Annapolis, Maryland
E-mail: go to web site for on-line form
Web: *www.nadn.navy.mil/*
Phone: 410-293-4361

U.S. Merchant Marine Academy, Kings Point, New York
E-mail: *admissions@usmma.edu*
Web: *www.usmma.edu/admissions/*
Phone: 800-732-6267

U.S. Coast Guard Academy, New London, Connecticut
E-mail: *admissions@cga.uscg.mil*
Web: *www.cga.edu/*
Phone: 860-444-8500

CHAPTER 3

MONEY TALKS—
AND THE
CONVERSATIONS
ARE HEAVY-DUTY

R emember when your high school student was born and you said, "We've got to start saving for college right away"? Well, "right away" is right now. You don't need to panic, but you do need to hunker down and figure out your game plan(s).

COLLEGE FINANCING CHATS

"We told our children we would pay for costs for a state school education. So one went to a state school and his way was paid. The other went to a private college and we paid the amount it would have cost for a state school education at that time. He made up the difference himself."

Elaine Gingerich

"We told our daughter she could go to Loyola, but I'd never visit her there because I'd be working three jobs to pay the tuition."

Rose Kelly

"One college was wooing our son so hard with a great scholarship that we backed away from giving input. We even paid fancy fees to a college guidance advisor who focused only on the academic, not the total living environment and how it would suit our child's personality. In the end, he stayed at that particular college two years. It was totally wrong for him. We went back to our own parameters for the next child."

Jay Welch

Obviously, money is an issue, but it shouldn't be the only issue. Choosing a college that is a good match with your child is crucial because of the growing, getting along, and maturing that accompany the academics.

Talk enough about college costs in front of your child so that the youngster begins to understand that there really isn't a tree out back busily growing dollar bills. But don't talk too much about college costs in front of your child, or he may back away from going because of the burden (or perceived burden) it would place upon the family.

Sit down at the kitchen table with your kid and a big bowl of popcorn to talk about how your student will be expected to provide some of the money for this education venture, whether it's for tuition, room and board, or simply for spending.

Be up front with your expectation that the child will finish college in four years, or five if that is the program requirement. Many students take five years to graduate from state universities because of the unavailability of classes. Say how much money you can provide and for how long.

Help your child visualize the long-term effects of building up a huge debt from college costs. Discuss how many years it could take to pay off such a debt, especially with interest added, and how that debt could affect job choices.

And all the while, know that financing a college education is not a topic your student is particularly interested in discussing.

"We told our daughters we would cover college expenses, but they'd have to raise spending money. Everything went fine until Christmas break. By then, one daughter had an entrepreneur boyfriend who believed that the way you became an entrepreneur was to sit around and think about working instead of actually working. So our daughter chose not to work. Well, when it came time for her to go back to school, her father wouldn't give her any travel money. When she was two states away, she stopped driving long enough to call home and say, 'I just wanted you to know that I'm really sorry I left angry. Also, it's snowing out and I may never see you again.' She always worked after that."

Diane Lenahan

"We struck a deal with each of our kids. They were to earn as much scholarship money as they could, then pay the remaining costs from their freshman year after graduation. We'd pay for the other three years. However, we told them up front that three years was our limit. If they had to go longer, we wouldn't be paying the tuition. Every one of them made it in four years!"

Dennis Rhodes

FRANKLY, MY DEARS, WE DO GIVE A DARN— COSTS AND CHOICES

"We told our children they were on the four-year plan. They would have to work and earn all their spending money, but we'd support them otherwise for four years."

Jay Welch

"Money's always been big with our daughter, so we told her she would get a certain amount each month as long as she was in college. Then she discovered that her new roommate was going to be receiving $100 a month more from her parents. We said we were happy for her roommate. Our daughter went out and got a job in order to keep up with the room-mate."

Ben Brouhard

"We indicated the amount we could contribute each year toward college. Our daughter did the math, then asked, 'Where will I get the rest?'

'Student loans,' we replied.

'Loans? I'd have to pay them back! No way!' she said.

'Then start looking into state-supported schools,' we suggested. And so she did."

Janet Heimbuch

Check costs for each college or university, community college, technical school, or specialized school in the mix. The differences can be huge. For example, an art school can cost $14,000 a year, while an art major at a state university may be half that or less.

It costs less if your child attends a community college for two years to get basic classes, then transfers to a four-year program. Be careful in selection, however, as most two- and four-year institutions do not offer identical experiences.

Still, college is a lifetime investment; it may not always be the best choice to select the least expensive alternative.

Set certain financial criteria now. What if . . .

—your student wants to attend a state school in another state instead of enrolling in a comparable academic program close to home? Who pays the out-of-state tuition difference?
—your student decides to move from the dorm to a more expensive apartment? Who pays the difference?
—your student believes he will need ten sweaters and you believe he will need five? Who pays the difference?
—your student spends three years in engineering classes, then announces she's switching to a philosophy major? Who pays the difference?

Sometimes room and board bills for the dorm and cafeteria are higher than for an apartment and the grocery store.

The issue may not be how much money you have to spend so much as how you choose to spend the money you have. Will your child do better in a large or small school? Close to home or far away? In a state university or a private college?

An important part of the college experience is living away from home. If there's a college in your hometown, this can become a point of discussion as you consider finances.

Some parents send their child to a less expensive undergraduate school so they can help with graduate school costs. But most parents say, "It's your dime for graduate school."

Luckily, conventional wisdom and lots of parents believe freshmen have all they can do to achieve academically and socially. At best, a car is a neutral factor and, more likely, a negative one. Providing a car for your college freshman can add significantly to your costs, and your list of worries. Besides, constantly looking for a parking spot, or dodging parking tickets as the case may be, is a nuisance. In fact, some schools don't allow freshmen to bring cars to campus.

"Our son had surgery during his freshman year of college, so he needed a car for six weeks to get back and forth for rehab. I told him it was 24 miles a trip for rehab and that we'd be checking the odometer when we picked the car back up after the six weeks were over."

Cathy Sweeney

FINANCIAL OPTIONS—LET US COUNT THE WAYS

"We started saving for college the year my husband began working. A salesman friend of his suggested we set up a college fund. That was $15 a month starting in 1964—at the time a lot for us to put away. But it helped tremendously."

Karen Shroyer

"We have been married for 33 years, and decided if there were ever going to be a divorce, it would be over financial aid forms. If you skip one line on that form, it all comes back on you and your child is back in the house again."

Rose Kelly

Here's one for the planning-*way*-ahead department: See if your state schools offer any advance payment tuition plans. It could mean your child's tuition would be paid for by the time your youngster first steps on campus. Of course, there are lots of different plans, so check with a financial aid professional to understand all the consequences before enrolling.

For most parents, paying tuition and room and board are huge challenges. Still, they'll tell you they "just keep on keepin' on" as far as earning enough money to get their child through college is concerned. In fact, parents say it seems like you don't do anything but pay college expenses for four (or five) years.

Maybe you don't eat out as often, or you stop buying junk food. Maybe you rent videos instead of going to the movies. Maybe you rearrange the furniture to cover up worn carpeting instead of going to the floor-covering store—discounts notwithstanding! Maybe you discover the pleasures of long walks in the park, reading books borrowed from the library, and following up on every free event listed in the Sunday newspaper's arts section!

And still you'll probably have to borrow unless you find that you really do have a rich uncle. Just be sure to borrow enough to cover everything, including those hidden expenses listed under The Twilight Zone of College Financing—Hidden Costs, page 63. Then, when the end-of-the-year bill arrives with a zero-cents balance due, you'll feel happy, like somebody just gave you a present, even though you know you paid for it.

Some families have a pot of money set aside to pay for college. If the pot's empty about the same time the kid gets his diploma, the parents shrug and say, "Well, can you think of a better investment we could have made?" Others put a lump sum into savings every year. The trick is to keep the money there until the youngster actually starts college!

Paying for college is like paying off three mortgages, but only living in one house. You give one third of your money to Uncle Sam, one third to the college, and one third to yourself. Except most parents don't recall ever seeing that third third.

Some pay for the whole year up front, which causes them to eat beans and rice until June. Others go the monthly payment route, which helps the cash flow, or at least slows the bleeding from borrowing a lot all at once.

Actually, there are lots of options. Contact the school's financial aid office after your child is accepted and ask for assistance.

Don't plan on your kid snagging a big sports, activity, or academic scholarship based on abilities demonstrated to date. Better to be surprised than disappointed.

Get (free!) scholarship information from the school guidance counselor. Most is updated annually. Also, log on to the Internet, go to the public library and bookstores, and call college admissions offices. Be wary of companies that offer a list of guaranteed scholarships for a fee.

You may require your child to pay a portion of the Big Bill. In most cases, that means the student takes out a loan, incurs debt, then works hard to pay it off later. Is that so bad?

To an 18-year-old, a $2,500 loan is like *"Wow!"* and *"Yikes!"* Your child understands that, at some point, she must pay it back. She may also understand that paying it back will be easier if she has that degree.

VOICES OF EXPERIENCE

"We never went to college so we had no experience to draw on. We actually weren't aware of any type of financial assistance. Plus with us working two different job shifts, there was no time to talk about what we might do."

Cathy Sweeney

"As a single parent, I started saving the year before my daughter went to college. I said she'd go even if I had to get three jobs—and I did. Actually, with financial aid for academics, there was enough for a state school. But I told her to decide what she needed to succeed—and she said an all-girls private school because it had small classes and she wouldn't be in competition for boys' attention. She thought looks were too important at a coed school. So she went to the all-girls school and who knows? Maybe she wouldn't have made it in another setting."

Sheila Ayala

AND THE GOOD NEWS IS—DOLLAR DEALS

- Used textbooks will be cheaper than new ones, and even used ones are ridiculously expensive. But they sell like hotcakes. Go early. Shop quickly.
- Do chain or local bookstores carry any of the required textbooks? They may be cheaper there than in the college bookstore. But don't assume

that, because college students always complain about prices at the university bookstore.

- And, of course, price check Amazon.com, Powells.com, and other Internet vendors. Remember to add in delivery charges, which can make the cheaper book ultimately more expensive. The return process is more complicated, too.

- You know that generic over-the-counter and prescription drugs are cheaper than brand names, but we'll bet that's news to your child.

- Kids like to buy clothes at the Salvation Army, not necessarily because it's a good way to save money, but because everybody else does. Whatever! It's easy on the pocketbook.

- Some colleges offer free or reduced tuition for employees and dependents at that college, or at others with which it has reciprocal agreements. But the rules usually are strict and just because you work at the college doesn't mean you'll get a tuition rebate. It's worth asking about, though, if you happen to be in the job market before your child's senior year of high school.

- State college tuition for students who live out of state can rival private college tuition. But some state schools' rules defining an in-state resident make it possible for out-of-staters to eventually qualify as in-state residents and get that cheaper tuition. Plus, some public colleges offer in-state tuition to the children of alumni who live out of state.

- Some airlines, trains, and buses offer student travel coupons or fares for travel within the United States. The deals may not be as good as discount fares, but kids can get home without breaking the budget if there's a family emergency.

- Check into all the angles for cheaper transportation. Then check again and again because fares are constantly changing.

- Become friends with the Internet to check fares and special deals.

- Inquire about transportation coupons for students and parents visiting colleges during the search process.

- Bus companies sometimes offer 30-day travel passes with reduced fares.

- Some transportation companies offer coupons buried deep within those catalogs you don't order but get anyway. Or the coupons may arrive in conjunction with a product promotion. Moral: Start checking your junk mail!

- Airline tickets generally are less expensive if purchased ahead of time. How far ahead? Oh, sometimes 30 days, sometimes 21. The requirement is like a moving target.

- If you buy a ticket ahead of time and there's an airfare war, you may exchange the ticket for a less expensive one and receive the residual difference in the form of a travel voucher. However, that assumes the first ticket is refundable. Plus, you'll pay a hefty change fee.

- Along with transportation deals, additional discounts may be available at restaurants, entertainment hot spots, and, of course, retail stores.

- All this purchase-of-tickets talk assumes that your child knows when she'll be coming home. That's often not the case. For example, even though most schools publish the final exam schedule at the beginning of the semester, most students won't be aware of it until about 36 hours before the tests begin. Since they can't travel home until the last exam is over, purchasing a ticket ahead of time can be folly. Finding a decently priced ticket in such a short time is out of the question. Alternatively, desperate parents might check the college's web site for the exam schedule and discuss possibilities with your student.

- If you give your student your travel agent's 800 number so he can make his own transportation arrangements, you'll find out when he's coming home because the agent will call you for your credit card number to pay for the ticket.

- Once they have a ticket, some students have turned getting bumped from a flight in return for free travel vouchers into an art form.

- Ask if the college accepts credit card payments for tuition, room and board, and other bills. Then, if your credit card awards frequent flyer miles, you just might cash in those miles and go sit on a beach somewhere to celebrate after commencement.

- Obviously, carpools save money but the wear-and-tear on parents' nerves may not be worth it. Long-distance driving to most of these kids means heading to work or the video store. And college kids pack so much stuff into a car before taking a trip that the driver's range of vision is more like a straight shot out the front windshield. Period.

VOICES OF EXPERIENCE

"Our son called to say he was riding home with a couple of kids over spring break. I said, 'No! You catch the plane home. I don't want you on the highway with a bunch of teenagers.' Unbeknownst to me, my son rode home with these kids anyway. The kids got home during the middle of a party we were hosting. I

left my guests to go talk to them. I asked how the trip went. The girl who drove said nonchalantly, 'The trip was fine, but I did get a speeding ticket.' I was livid! She said she was not going that fast. I said if she was going over the posted speed limit, it was too fast. That's why it's called a speed limit!' "

Paula Dawson

THE TWILIGHT ZONE OF COLLEGE FINANCING—HIDDEN COSTS

"Add up all the extra costs such as a waste basket, clothes hamper, light bulbs, a desk lamp, a fan—they mount up. After my sons enrolled, I'd send goodies, and I found out I was not only feeding my boys but also a whole lot of their dorm friends. That does add to good PR in the dorm community!"

Diana Pace

"Our biggest bill was $700 for two months' worth of phone calls our son made to us and his friends. He had an access code in the dorm and I guess he thought the calls were free. I wrapped the canceled check up with the bill, marked it in big red letters, 'PAID IN FULL, Merry Christmas, Love from Mom and Dad,' and that was his present. His only present. It was a very difficult thing for me to do."

Cathy Sweeney

Count the hidden costs before making a final selection. A large city costs more than a rural setting, but air transportation to rural areas is higher. The farther away from home the school is, the more transportation will cost. And, cold weather locations mean winter clothes, which are more expensive than shorts and sandals.

Can your youngster get the degree in four years? As previously mentioned, sometimes state schools are tight on space, and students can't get the classes they need to graduate on time. If it will take your youngster five years to get a degree from a state school, will the final cost be equivalent to four years at a private college? (Remember, out-of-state students usually pay much higher tuition than in-state students at public colleges.) Also, factor in that your child will not be earning income for another year.

If the goal is to graduate in four years, make sure your kid emblazons the credit requirements on her forehead. That includes physical education, which students are notorious for ignoring until it's way too late.

Factor in costs for computer and printer, program and/or lab fees, art materials, entertainment, travel, eating out (kids can take just so much dining hall food before their bodies walk themselves to a pizza joint), phone bills, club activities, joining the Greek system, cleaning supplies, bedding, materials to build a loft in the dorm room, posters—hear the cash register ringing?

STUDY ABROAD

Let's say your kid calls home announcing, "Everybody's going abroad next fall. If you don't send me, too, I'll be the only one left on campus!" Despite that dramatic exaggeration, a fair number of students do study abroad, usually in their junior year. Your costs may be about the same whether your child is here or there, except for that plane ticket to get across the pond.

If your youngster wants to go overseas with a program sponsored by a college other than his own or by a consortium to which his college doesn't belong, you may need to look for more money under the mattress.

Or your student may find a cheaper study-abroad program than her school offers. Bottom line: Check costs for different programs and the college's class credit rules.

Some schools allow students to apply their financial aid to the study-abroad experience, especially if the program is affiliated with the student's university.

ONE RINGY-DINGY . . .

Often, colleges assign telephone access codes, which are unique to each student in the dormitory. The code enables the student to get an outside line that connects to a long-distance carrier. Access codes eliminate direct billing. Evidently, they also make it difficult for the student to remember that the calls cost money, although parents are painfully reminded of that when the bill arrives in their mail.

Get an 800 phone number for your youngster to use when calling home, but don't pay for your student's calls to friends. (This is not considered cruel and unusual punishment.)

Realize that for an 800 number to work, your student must not only remember what the number is, but he also must remember to use it. Simply knowing the number exists is not enough.

A student who has a problem remembering his 800 number should not jot it down on the hallway wall outside his dorm room.

Both 800 numbers and regular long-distance calls cost money. E-mail is almost always free through the college.

Which brings up another consideration: Are Internet charges included in room and board? What about cable TV charges?

Other clever ways to keep the costs down:

- Score high on Advanced Placement tests and you may automatically receive college credits for those courses.
- Take a college course or two while still in high school and, in some states, the school district will foot the bill.
- "CLEP" out of college courses by scoring satisfactorily on one or more of 34 CLEP (College-Level Examination Program) exams. More than 2,800 colleges and universities award CLEP credits.

Know the rules before you start playing the game. Some schools offer interim courses between semesters or during winter break. They may not be included in the regular tuition fee, which would mean yet another peek under the mattress.

SPRING BREAK

It's hard to imagine at this point in the college planning process, but spring break may easily become a "hidden cost."

Spring Break Dialogue:

Parent: "You come home for spring break and we'll pay your way. Go somewhere else for spring break and you pay your way."

Child: "How about you pay me what it would cost to come home for spring break and I'll apply that to my trip to Cancun? I wouldn't want you to waste the money you set aside."

"I'M STARVING!"

You can sign 'em up for the breakfast-lunch-dinner meal plan and you still get desperate phone calls from your student who is "starving to death!" You ask, "Isn't the cafeteria open? Don't they have a salad bar? Didn't I send you overnight food packed in dry ice?" In response, they simply moan weakly.

Even if your child goes on the full food plan, you have to spend $50 or $100 at the grocery store every time you visit campus because everybody else's parents do. Know that once the food is unpacked back in the dorm room, there will be kids running up and down the hall and hollering, "So-and-so has food!"

Tell your child that you're not going to buy the whole meal plan next year if she isn't going to use it, and suddenly, the cafeteria food won't look so bad.

"I'M (COUGH, COUGH) SICK"

One other cost you don't think about: health insurance. College kids don't eat right, they sleep funny hours, they get stressed out. And they get sick. So, who's gonna pay the doctor?

Every state has different laws and every insurance company has different rules. You need to know the rules that apply to your youngster. For instance, will your family policy pay as much for out-of-state as in-state health care? Are part-time students over 18 still covered by a family policy? What's the cut-off age for student coverage? Does your policy cover visits to student health services or an infirmary? We don't know. Better call your insurance company.

It's imperative that somebody in the family understands this insurance thing so your youngster doesn't end up uninsured.

The college's health insurance plan may or may not be better than the health coverage you already carry on your child. Carefully read the information the college provides, because your kid won't read it at all.

If you decide to purchase the school insurance, do it before your youngster moves onto campus and suffers a torn anterior cruciate ligament in the knee that requires surgery and months of supervised rehabilitation.

Does the college offer insurance that protects your semester's payments in case your student must drop out for any number of specified reasons? (Flunking out doesn't count.) Then those payments can be applied to the semester the student returns.

Come the end of freshman year, you'll find one last hidden cost. Remember all that stuff you hauled off to campus in the fall? First, you will groan, then you will need to decide whether it's cheaper to haul it all back home again or to rent storage space on campus. Just like everything else, either way it's going to cost you.

VOICES OF EXPERIENCE

"I'll give you an example of hidden costs. Our daughter called from school saying she couldn't possibly drive home unless the stereo speakers in the car were fixed first. We negotiated with her regarding how much we were willing to pay to fix the speakers."

Julie Brouhard

"Once our son used his [cafeteria] swipe card for breakfast, but he was in a hurry so he only got a cup of coffee. Then, he came back after class and tried to order his real breakfast. The cafeteria worker told him he'd have to use his swipe card, and he said he'd done that earlier to get a cup of coffee. The worker replied, 'Well, then, you've already had breakfast.'"

Cathy Sweeney

"My daughter's first phone bill was $300 and I didn't pay it. I talked to the school's business office and asked them not to accept my daughter's code for two months. She started doing e-mail."

Sheila Ayala

MONEY MANAGEMENT 101—A LESSON YOUR STUDENT NEEDS NOW

VOICES OF EXPERIENCE

"I think when kids are held responsible for certain expenditures, they become much more reasonable about managing money. They understand that in addition to eating dorm food, they can order pizza at night. But they think twice about calling the delivery person."

Karen Dakin

"Our kids received an allowance since they were old enough to walk. We had a list of chores on the refrigerator, and if they didn't do their chores, they lost their allowance. Also, if they wanted a pair of $75 shoes, we'd offer to pay $30 of it. Then, they had a choice of whether to get that pair and pay the extra, go with a lesser non-name for our dollar value, or pick a compromise. Then, they didn't want the shoes anymore."

Daniel Lazzaro

Odd but true: One kid handles money like it's confetti to throw on a parade; his sibling hoards money like she's afraid of the return of the Great Depression. Go figure.

Although nobody gets a free ride, there may be a few free short jaunts along the way. Especially when Mother thinks, "That's my baby. I'll just slip him $50 in the mail." Or when Father decides, "I'm going to send $25 to our daughter," then ends up writing the check for $50.

Note that in the previous situation, a student almost always gets either a mother or a father like that, but never both. Not having two quietly generous parents cuts down on the student's income, but it does create a pretty nice system of checks-and-balances back home.

Talking to your child about the importance of developing and following a budget will be easy. Getting your child to actually listen to you will *not* be easy. Getting him to write down a budget will be next to impossible.

If you haven't already begun making your child responsible for earning, spending, and saving money, better late than never:

1. Take your child to the bank so he can open a savings account. Depending on your child's maturity level, you may also want him to open up a checking account. Explain that if the account goes below a certain amount, he—not you—will have to pay the bank's penalty charge.
2. Once that high school graduation money starts rolling in, encourage your child to deposit at least some of it in the savings account.
3. Do your tax returns with your high school student, or go over the completed return together.
4. Start discussing investment possibilities. This will excite some young people and cause others' eyes to glaze over.
5. Discuss your student's health insurance benefits. Make sure she understands how she is covered, what that coverage involves, how to use the insurance card, and all the hoop-jumping that actually using the card will involve. You don't want to receive a $1,000 bill in the mail because your kid didn't go to the right place for medical treatment.

Part of Money Management 101 (the hard part) will be watching your child make small mistakes with his hard-earned money. Also hard will be explaining afterward how a different approach would have worked better. Of course, you could just fix the mistakes yourself. Again and again and again.

WHERE'S THE CASH?

Discuss how your kid can get his hands on cold, hard cash once he's on campus. What about a money machine? It allows students to retain their hometown bank account—an attractive option if the money machine is affiliated with that bank and is centrally located. But will there be transaction fees?

What about opening a bank account in the college town? But will there be check fees and/or a minimum monthly fee?

Potpourri advice: Estimate how many checks your child will write in a semester, then determine what those check fees will be at a hometown bank versus what they would cost at the campus town bank. Also, estimate money machine charges versus the cost of using a credit card. Which is less? Which is more convenient? Is the convenience worth paying extra?

CHARGE IT!

What about a credit card? Credit card companies look under every rock in the college dorm for new customers, so you'll need to talk about why signing up for all the offers that come along isn't a good idea. But is your youngster disciplined enough to buy on credit?

Regardless, set limits on the card's use. Perhaps it can be used only for books, supplies, and travel. (Some college stores provide a charge account for books and whatever else you buy there.) Oh, okay, and maybe use the card to get dress shoes for the dance.

If your child does well with one credit card, her positive record of on-time payments becomes a powerful tool later on. Also, it's almost a must when your youngster is traveling.

If you opt for the credit card route and your youngster treats money like confetti, have his credit card bill sent to your home address, with the understanding that you will be opening it each month. That doesn't teach responsibility, but it might prevent filing for bankruptcy.

Some students never need Money Management 101 because they're able to get other people to buy everything for them. Quite frankly, we don't know how they do that.

A Money Management 101 lesson for parents: The first year that your child is gone, you'll spend a lot of time by the phone, just in case she calls needing something. By the time she's a sophomore, you'll realize that the only thing she needs is more money. Consequently, you may put some distance between yourself and that phone.

VOICES OF EXPERIENCE

"My daughter opened an account with the bank before she left for college. Within six months, she received a letter from the bank saying she was $330 overdrawn. I told her the two things most important in your life were a good education and good credit. I said that you can have all this cash, but without a good credit history, you will not get many things. It always comes down to your credit history."

Sheila Ayala

"Our daughter worked all summer and saved $1,000 for her spending money. Necessities like concert tickets, university sweatshirts, sorority favors, beer mugs, etcetera, soon whittled down her account. Spring came and with only three weeks to go, she called and told us her account was depleted. I sent her the only two things I thought she really needed: Tampax and toothpaste. The next phone call home, she told us she was waitressing at the country club while studying for finals. Kids learn to be creative problem solvers if you don't rescue them."

Joyce Pope

FINANCIAL AID: SOMETHING FOR ALMOST EVERYONE

The easiest way to pay for college is to pluck whatever amount you need from the money tree out back. If, for some reason, that doesn't work, phone your rich uncle (or aunt). If that doesn't work either, apply for financial aid. Thousands of families just like yours are applying right this minute. As a matter of fact, very few families pay all of their child's college education expenses without assistance.

Here's what you need to know about qualifying for financial aid:

FREE APPLICATION FOR FEDERAL STUDENT AID
(www.fafsa.ed.gov)

To qualify for most federal and institutional financial aid programs, you must first complete a Free Application for Federal Student Aid (FAFSA). You'll provide your income, net worth, federal tax return information, family size, and number of family members in college. Children of divorced parents need to ask a financial aid officer about reporting what from whom on the FAFSA. Even in a remarriage where a prenuptial agreement stipulates that the stepparent not pay for college, that stepparent's income will be figured into the mix.

A processor then determines how much both you and your student may reasonably be expected to pay toward the education. (Students are positive that their share is "way too high!") Those two contributions represent your Expected Family Contribution, which remains fairly constant from one school to another.

Schools download your Expected Family Contribution information, then deduct that amount from the school's costs for tuition, books, fees, and living expenses to determine your student's eligibility for loans, grants, and scholarships, which make up the financial aid package. Your amount of "need" will vary from one school to another, depending on how much each school costs.

Some (sort of) good news: Schools can make adjustments in your contribution because of unusual medical or dental expenses, tuition expenses for children in private elementary or secondary school, or if you, your spouse, or either of your parents (if applicable) have been recently unemployed. Conversely, if you win the lottery, expect schools to make adjustments in the other direction.

FAFSA forms are available after December 1, but don't submit them until after January 1, when you have gathered your tax information for the previous year. Actual due dates vary; some states and institutions give priority consideration to forms received by a certain date. Those students will be considered for certain types of financial aid before those whose forms arrive after that date. Priority consideration is important since—surprise!—aid does not pour forth from a bottomless pit. You may have to submit estimated tax figures in the FAFSA to meet those earlier deadlines. Then, you'll re-file corrected figures to FAFSA when your tax returns are complete.

There are several ways to submit a FAFSA:

- Using FAFSA on the Internet at *www.fafsa.ed.gov* is one way. You need a personal computer or a Macintosh that is equipped with a supported browser. Also, you can check the status of your application on the Web.

- Using FAFSA Express, a free software program that allows you to apply from your home computer or a computer at a central location like your high school, a college, or a public library. It can be used only on a personal computer equipped with the Windows operating system and a modem. You can also order FAFSA Express on diskette by calling 1-800-801-0576 (TDD 1-800-511-5806).

- Having your school submit your application electronically.

- Mailing a paper FAFSA.

Note that with electronic application, you may also need to mail in a signature page.

And then? Within a week of receiving an on-line FAFSA, the U.S. Department of Education will send results in a Student Aid Report; the Department's response to snail mail takes three to four weeks. You'll read the report, discover how much you may be reasonably expected to pay, scream "What!!?" and faint.

When you regain consciousness, here are three thoughts to mull over:

1. The Expected Family Contribution on the Student Aid Report is referred to by professionals as "what you are expected to contribute." That also translates into "what you are able to pay," which may include what you are able to borrow.

2. Schools don't necessarily expect you to borrow. They're simply saying you are eligible to receive X amount of dollars. If their dollars and the dollars you already have aren't enough when combined to pay tuition, you'll need to explore other resources, such as finding money under the mattress or borrowing.

3. The Student Aid Report will never tell a family up front that it doesn't qualify for financial aid. But if you had to add another room onto the house just to stuff your money in, it's a sure bet that the schools will look at the FAFSA report and not offer a penny in aid.

In addition to the FAFSA, which has no application fee, most schools require your student to submit the school's financial aid application along with the admission application. There may be a fee for the school application. The school financial aid form is nothing like the FAFSA; in fact, your student may be able to complete it. About a week after students receive admittance letters, they receive financial aid packages. The packages usually consist of a combination of grants, loans, and work-study funds.

INDEPENDENT VERSUS DEPENDENT

"So," you say, "I'll declare my kid as an independent and then she'll be eligible for more financial aid!" That works only if the student:

—is 24 years of age or older, or
—is a veteran of the U.S. Armed Forces, or
—is a graduate or professional student, or
—is an orphan or a ward of the court, or
—is married, or
—has legal dependents other than a spouse.

But it was a good try, anyway.

THE CSS/FINANCIAL AID PROFILE

PROFILE is a program of the College Board, a national, nonprofit association of schools and school systems, colleges and universities, and educational organizations. Many colleges, universities, graduate and professional schools, and scholarship programs use the information collected on PROFILE to help them award nonfederal student aid funds.

Here's how PROFILE works:

1. Register for your application at *www.collegeboard.org* by clicking on the PROFILE icon. Then, you can either complete the application immediately (which will require a credit card), or request the paper version be sent to you.

2. Or register by calling 1-800-778-6888 if you live in the United States, Puerto Rico, or Canada. If you live elsewhere, call 1-305-816-2550. You'll receive an application within seven to ten working days.

3. Once your application has been processed, you'll receive an acknowledgment showing the schools and programs to which your information will be sent. The report may also contain information from your schools and programs about the next steps in the process. Also, you can ask the College Board to send your information to additional schools and programs.

When should you register? As soon as you are sure about where you are applying for aid. The completed application must be returned at least two weeks before the earliest priority filing date specified by your schools and programs. "Priority filing date" means the date by which the school or program tells you that the College Board must receive your completed application. Such dates are provided on-line or in the letter that accompanies your application packet.

How much does this cost? A nonrefundable $7 registration fee ($6 if registration is on-line), plus $16 for each school or program to which you want information sent. There may be some limited additional charges.

Can you use PROFILE to apply for federal student aid? Nope.

Wanna know more? E-mail questions to *help@cssprofile.org* or call 1-305-829-9793 or TDD at 1-800-915-9990.

GRANTS

Grants do not need to be repaid. Some are awarded on the basis of academic ability or talent; others require that your child provide some type of service, such as participating in the school's athletic or music programs.

—Federal Pell Grants are awarded to high-need undergraduates who will be or are in eligible institutions. Pell Grants provide a financial aid "foundation" to which aid from other federal and nonfederal sources can be added.

—Federal Supplemental Educational Opportunity Grants (FSEOG) go to students whose needs are greater than those targeted by the Pell Grant program. Amounts are determined by the college or university.

—Miscellaneous other federal grants are available for students who meet specific requirements.

—States also award grants but, among other requirements, the recipients must attend college within that state to collect the grant.

LOANS

Loans must be repaid over a prearranged time period.

—Federal Family Education Loan Program (FFELP) provides long-term, low-interest loans to students and parents. Your student must be enrolled or accepted for enrollment at least halftime at a participating institution.

—Federal Direct Loan Program (FDLP) is similar to the FFELP. The U.S. Department of Education is the lender and delivers the loan through the educational institution.

—Federal Stafford Loans aren't awarded until the school determines the student's eligibility for a Pell Grant, which also determines eligibility for a subsidized Stafford. On a subsidized, need-based Stafford Loan, the federal government pays the interest while the student is in school or has received a deferment, which can be given for a number of reasons. On a non-need-based or unsubsidized loan, the holder of the loan pays the interest during in-school and deferment periods.

—Federal Parent Loans for Undergraduate Students (PLUS) provide a certain amount of money per year for each of your dependent children enrolled in undergraduate school, regardless of need.

—Carl D. Perkins Loans are low-interest federal loans made directly to needy students.

—Private loan programs are available through many financial institutions, as you well know by now.

OTHER SOURCES

While the largest sources of aid are the federal, state, and local governments, aid also is available from private institutions, civic organizations, and academic and educational institutions.

—Scholarships, like grants, do not need to be repaid although they may require your child to perform some type of service. There are two types of scholarship: need-based, which is awarded because of the family's limited financial resources, and merit-based, which is awarded because of the student's academic ability or talent. Scholarship information is readily available and free. It's not necessary to "purchase" the information, although there are some folks out there more than willing to sell it to you.

—The Hope Scholarship Credit provides a nonrefundable tax credit of 100 percent of the first $1,000 and 50 percent of the next $1,000 for each of the first two years of postsecondary tuition and fees (but not books, room, or board). The maximum annual credit is $1,500. Your student(s) must be enrolled on at least a half-time basis in a program leading to a degree, certificate, or other recognized educational credential in an eligible institution.

—Work-study programs provide full- or part-time employment while your student is in school. The Federal College Work-Study Program (CWS) gives preference to students with the greatest financial need. Because any work-study program usually is part of a financial package, you'll have to come up with that particular sum of money if your student chooses not to participate.

—AmeriCorps, a national service program, provides money either as a tuition voucher or repayment of a loan to persons who have worked one year with communities in the areas of education, environment, human interaction, and public safety.

—Qualifying students can receive assistance through the Veteran's Administration and Vocational Rehabilitation Programs.

—All branches of the Armed Forces offer the Montgomery GI Bill, which helps enlistees pay education costs.

—There are more grants and scholarships from private clubs, associations, and businesses than you can shake a stick at. It may take some digging, but hard workers are able to nickel, dime, and dollar their way through a fair amount of the tuition payments.

—Don't overlook internships and cooperative education where students can work part-time in fields in which they are interested. In other words, look under every rock.

—When the tax man cometh, tell him you're putting a kid through college. You may be eligible to claim a Federal Tax Credit against federal income taxes. Call 1-800-4FED-AID or TDD 1-800-730-8913.

Detailed information regarding financial aid should be available through your school counselor or college financial aid offices within state government. Often such state agencies present parent seminars, as do colleges and high schools.

EVALUATING THE OFFERS

Compare the financial aid package offers from each college. It's not necessarily true that the higher priced the school, the bigger your bill will be. Although your FAFSA Expected Family Contribution may remain fairly constant from one school to another, many other factors come into play. Generally, the more expensive schools offer larger financial aid packages, so the bottom line becomes not the total amount of aid you receive, but the amount of money you will have to pay or repay in the form of loans.

Also, the biggest award may not always be the best. Note:

—how much of each package is scholarship or grant money, which doesn't have to be repaid, and how much is a loan, which does;
—the terms and obligations of each loan;
—whether work-study is included (Will your student have time for that and still do well in class?);
—whether your student will be able to get all the classes needed to graduate in four years;
—the scholarship terms (some renew automatically, some only under certain conditions, and some not at all);
—how much your student can be expected to earn in the first years after graduation, especially if your student will be paying off some or all of the loans.

And finally: Don't forget about paying back what you owe later. (Later, as you know, will be here sooner than you think.) Terms to be familiar with are:

—Forbearance: a temporary postponement or reduction of payments.
—Deferment: an approved postponement of payment for a specified time.
—Consolidation: combining existing student loans into one new loan, which generally results in lower monthly payments but higher total interest costs.

Like a giant squid with endless, waving tentacles, the Internet reaches into almost every part of the get-into-college scene. Not surprisingly, colleges, kids—and sometimes parents, too—are going high tech. Here are some tips about on-line information for colleges, standardized tests, and applications.

CONNECTING WITH ALL COLLEGES—LITERALLY

> "One thing hasn't changed with computers and the college information search: Parents still need to supervise the process, not control it."
>
> Susie Polden

Your youngsters probably are right about this much: They *are* smarter than you—on the Internet, anyway.

So do yourself a favor: Know the "address" of the sites you want to visit on the Web before you head into cyberspace. Some say there's more junk than helpful information on the Web, and it's easy to get lost. The addresses you need will be in books and, most likely, on the tip of the high school guidance counselor's tongue.

It's a good thing kids know how to surf so well, because they can do just about anything on-line from submitting an application to learning whether they were accepted or rejected.

Most colleges have web sites that contain everything those pretty paper brochures do and more. Course descriptions, faculty profiles, activities, off-campus life, video tours, links to the community and local newspaper—enough to keep a person glued on-screen through a whole football season. Students quickly can request information be sent via USPS.

Then there are the alternative sites for colleges, those that are not authorized or maintained by colleges but offer a whale of a lot of information from rants to raves. Of course, either way, just because such sites exist doesn't mean the information accurately portrays the college.

With software programs usually available in guidance offices or commercially, students can search by various criteria such as size, major, or geographic area. If you know you want your child to stay within 500 miles of home, it's a quick way to narrow the search.

Most school guidance offices have college search software for computers, which you can use by yourself or with your student. Surprisingly, some kids actually like going to their folks' workplace and searching together on the computer.

Kids are regular Van Cliburns on the computer keys, so the faster a college web site "loads" (in other words, appears completely viewable), the more likely the college may be to find a place on your student's Long, Meandering List of Colleges. And if the site is hard or slow to "navigate" (get to various topics), the school may be history in 30 seconds.

In fact, your youngster can surf so fast through the postsecondary world that you may not even know what college sites he has visited. So talk with him early on about how much involvement you'd like in the search process. Parents can surf, too, you know.

In addition to individual college web sites, other sites offer answers to just about everything you could possibly ask about the SAT, ACT, scholarships, and loans (see Appendix, Resources). Some sites allow students to fill out personal profiles that include high school classes, interests, test scores, and grades. The profiles may be forwarded to colleges students select. Then watch for the mail blizzard!

Even with pounds of information from computer searches spread all over your youngster's room, still go to college fairs in the fall to start making face-to-face contacts with representatives.

Some college information sites have chat rooms or pages of comments from other parents. They can be, well, chatty. How much free time do you have anyway?

Realize that you're not chatting about your child with your best friend when you are on-line. Don't use your name, your child's name, or anything else that can identify your family.

Before taking any chat room tips to heart, discuss them with people you know.

VOICES OF EXPERIENCE

"My son e-mailed back and forth to kids he knew at various colleges or with friends who had older siblings in college. He'd say, 'I know your brother is going to such-and-such a school.' He may not have called them with questions, but he would e-mail them."

Audrey Valhuerdi

FINANCIAL AID, SCHOLARSHIPS, AND TESTS— PUSH-BUTTON ANSWERS

VOICES OF EXPERIENCE

"My youngster put off registering for the SAT until the last evening (before the deadline). Then she spent three hours trying to get on-line. She even called a guidance counselor to make sure she had to do it that evening. 'Unless you want to pay a $15 late fee, you do,' the counselor said. So my daughter kept at it and registered on time."

David Hafner

Guidance counselors usually address specific topics in presentations to classes of tenth, eleventh and twelfth graders. They'll probably give students a list of web sites for information on careers, applications, financial aid—the whole gamut. Parents may never see the information unless they ask!

Many web sites offer worksheets to calculate how much money college will cost and how many nights you'll spend barbecuing in the backyard instead of eating in a five-star restaurant. Also, some personal accounting programs help figure college cost projections.

Of course, parents should look at any financial aid web sites with their kids. First, students aren't all that interested in the money end of things. Second, they aren't as skeptical and attuned to scam possibilities.

Search the Web for scholarship opportunities. Just like off-line, though, if you are asked to pay big fees, watch your wallet; most of the information is available free in your high school counselor's office.

STANDARDIZED TESTS

Kids can register on-line for standardized tests for college admittance—the ACT at *www.act.org* and SAT at *www.collegeboard.org* are two such sites. Have the credit card handy, of course, and know the date and place you want to take the test. All that info is available on the site, or you can get a complete information packet from the school's guidance office.

As for test prep to master those tests, plenty of web sites and software are available to take you through the process. Methods include: simulated timed tests; interactive questions where the computer responds with why an answer is correct or incorrect, plus hints and strategies for solving math problems; drills; diagnosis of results; personalized study plans; and many other bells and whistles.

A wallet-friendly option: High school guidance offices usually have test practice software to be used at school.

Although kids can practice questions and tests as much as they want on computers, they can't take the real SAT and ACT on a computer. So be sure your youngster practices with the No. 2 pencil as well.

ON-LINE APPLICATION—IT'S EASY—CRASH!

"My son applied to one of his many college choices on-line. We could have done the same thing with his first choice college, but I felt uncomfortable. I thought: 'What if they don't get this? I push the send button and it's gone somewhere but I don't know where.' So we did that one by hand."

Paula Dawson

"In the high school library where I work, I noticed one girl was using the computer to apply to a college. I walked down to tell the counselors and they were surprised. The girl had told them she was not going to apply anywhere."

Claudia Harkins

Electronic applications aren't in the future. They're *now*. They're fast—which can be good *and* bad.

Computer applications allow the college to electronically connect your student with just about anybody on campus. For example, if your student toots her own horn in the high school band, the admissions office can connect her with the college band director. If she is from Anywhere, USA, and so are three students who already are at that school, the office can connect her with those students.

Computer apps sound handy for kids, too. After all, they can apply when they want, which is usually sometime after midnight. But they also can apply without the knowledge of or assistance from a parent or a counselor. That means they may skip all the steps about setting parameters and researching colleges first, and won't necessarily apply to schools that may be the best matches for them.

Kids can send multiple applications simply by typing in a particular school's code. Sometimes colleges even waive fees for electronic applications.

Just like preparing to take the SAT and ACT, the kids need to know the rules before they start. Watch them roll their eyes as you suggest they read the directions before filling out the on-line applications.

If the application calls for an identification number and password, tell your youngster to write them down. Then, when you think about all the places that paper could end up in his room, maybe you'll want to write them down, too.

Some things, such as teacher recommendations, must be submitted the traditional way in an envelope with a stamp and by a deadline. On the application checklist, which your child has printed out, have him highlight what must be collected and mailed separately.

WORD APPLICATION

It makes so much sense to write the essays in a word application such as Microsoft Word, WordPerfect, or Works. Editing is easier, plus some programs check your spelling and fix that grammar. Finally, you can copy and paste to the on-line application.

Many a word has been missed by the spell-check programs. *Their* tough to *sea* on *there* essays without a *print out*.

THE WEB PAGE

If your kid wants to study computer science or art, maybe she ought to figure out how to construct her own web page. If it's good, she should share the address on her college applications. If it mostly posts all the senior parties, though, best not to mention it.

Stranger than fiction: People post information on the web sites they wouldn't tell their own mother. Remind your computer whiz: If he doesn't want the world—and his mother—to know, don't put it on his web site.

BACKING UP AND PRINTING OUT

The cocky bird doesn't always get the worm, just dirt. So, urge your student to print out the application before transmitting it. Then she can proofread the application as a unit rather than as single screen pages.

Of course, on-line apps do not prevent students from procrastinating and spending hours trying to get on-line at the last moment to meet deadlines.

It's a given: Computer gremlins strike near those midnight deadlines and eat everything your child has entered as if it's a Dagwood Bumstead sandwich. So, here's the well-known and oft-ignored remedy: Back up everything after every session on the computer. It's a small price to pay for peace of mind.

Call it old-fashioned, but some parents just like to have the printout of the completed application in hand for the old-time accordion file. If the college responds electronically, print out the response, too.

Just like paper-and-pen applications, be sure to check with the college to ensure records, recommendations, and the check (if you didn't use a credit card) arrive and are credited to your student's file. Some colleges allow students to check on-line for the status of their application file.

Finally, call the college to discuss anything nonroutine about your youngster's application. For example, if the college waives classes when a student attains a particular AP score, call to be sure your youngster's AP class is properly credited, even though you know it should be okay.

"I know the computer is safe and reliable, but I felt safer with the U.S. Postal Service for his application. I just wanted to pay my $10.75 for express mail and see the application in the hands of the postal worker and know that it's really on the way."

Paula Dawson

"My son started an application at home on our old computer. It took a long time to download the application and it was frustrating. So he went to the community college where the computers were fast and did it quickly."

Claudia Harkins

A COMPUTER FOR COLLEGE—TO BUY OR NOT TO BUY

"We found that e-mail access was critical as soon as our daughter went away to college. She had free access to friends all over."

Nancy Johnson

"She kept in touch with her friends and it negated the homesickness factor."

John Johnson

"And it's invaluable for parents, too, because the kids actually e-mail you."

Daniel Lazzaro

"But when my daughter said she would write an e-mail thank-you note to Grandma, I said, 'No!' That's my e-mail line in the sand."

Kathy Hafner

Computers and college: like pizza and beer, an inseparable mix now on campuses everywhere.

Oh, the things college kids on computers can do. For starters, they:

—register for and change classes in minutes rather than stand and wait for hours in long lines;
—keep track of social engagements;
—take (*neat!*) notes in class;
—research paper topics;
—carry laptops to study groups and coffeehouses;
—take tests;
—visit on-campus chat rooms for classes or interest groups;
—participate in "paperless" classes where all assignments, work, and tests are communicated only via computer.

Of course, kids also play games and have a huge, active e-mail list for friends near and far. And they often e-mail parents. If for no other reason, it gives them an excuse to put off writing that term paper just a little longer.

Contrary to popular opinion, though, not every student wants a personal computer in college. Students who use the college's computer labs avoid concerns about what to purchase, repairs, crowding it into an already small room, and possible theft. Plus, you avoid friends who feel compelled to spend the night camped on your keyboard.

That may be enough pluses to have your student check out the college's computer labs before purchasing a computer. Note how many labs there are and where; hours open; how many, what kind, and how speedy the computers; and if technical assistance is available.

But also note whether the computer labs are jammed with students at crunch time when papers are due and whether there's 24-hour access, seven days a week. It could be ugly to have a paper due at 10:00 A.M. Monday but no lab access at 2:00 A.M. Monday.

COMPUTER DECISIONS

Ah, let us count the computer decisions: laptop or desktop, PC or Mac, faster or fastest? And that's just the beginning.

• For a laptop, add on decisions about a carrying case, surge protector, heavy-duty extension cord, and a monitor and keyboard to hook up to back in the dorm, not to mention the fact that those suckers are heavy. Will your student really want to lug the laptop all over campus?

• Find out if your student's computer paraphernalia will fit on the dormitory desk, or in some cases, even in the room. Is there room for two people's computer stuff and two hookups? And where will you store the computer during breaks, including summer?

- Who pays for Internet access? Is that included in the room cost? Then, is the Internet cost a factor when deciding whether it's cheaper to live in the dorm instead of moving off campus or to a Greek house?

- More questions: What if Susie Student talks to Sammie Student at lunch, and they walk off so engrossed in conversation about Pericles that they *forget* that their laptop computers are still under the table? And what if the computers disappear before Susie and Sammie finish their conversation? Check on an insurance policy or rider for laptop and for desktop computers in the dorm.

- Ask each college what kind of computer (Macintosh or PC) and software the school recommends, and if the school offers a discount purchase program. In fact, many schools mail out such information with the acceptance packet, including details about what's needed for Internet connection in the dorm room, where to purchase equipment, and the pros and cons of owning a laptop.

- Many colleges supply Internet connections to the buildings they own. There may be a charge for this, but it probably is a charge that everyone in a "wired" room has to pay. The college's computer network wires you directly to the Internet. However, your computer must meet certain standards to work.

- Off-campus students probably will need to subscribe to a commercial Internet service provider. Ask the college for directions to access university information.

- Often you can get a good deal at discount stores. But compare the gzillions of features and software packages that are bundled (in other words, come with) the computer. You might get a better buy elsewhere without the software your student will never use in this lifetime.

- A key question: You buy the computer at home, ship it 500 or 2,000 miles to college (let's just assume it arrives, undamaged), and your student uses it diligently until one night, all he can get on screen is a white line. Who's he gonna call to fix it?

- You can mail-order a computer, monitor, and printer to arrive at college with the youngster. Of course, some folks have horror stories: "They sent it to the wrong address" or "It never arrived and we had to order another one after the shipper couldn't find it." Lesson: Keep the paperwork with you and call the company the moment the computer is late in arriving.

- If your student is going into engineering, computer science, or graphics, she probably needs a faster computer than do English and history majors who write lots of papers. Check with the department professors for recommendations on speed and all that stuff. Your kid probably knows the jargon.

- If no one in the family knows anything about computers, check out computer magazines in bookstores or libraries. Some magazines rate computers and have explanations in ordinary English rather than "computereze."

- Maybe the family's computer can go to college with the student and you'll get a new computer at home. Why does it usually not work that way?

VOICES OF EXPERIENCE

"We investigated what kind of computer the college wanted, then bought each of our children a computer the summer before they went to college. We had them take training before leaving for school, plus their father gave them lessons. For example, he had them make spreadsheets for their bonds. It worked well, even for our son, who switched from business to education."

Cindy Finch

"Whether a personal computer—a laptop or 'hand-held' one—is essential depends on the kid's major. Hand-helds are essential for math, engineering, and other tech fields. Word processing can be done at a college computer center. Bottom line? It's nice to have an in-dorm room PC or laptop with printer in nontech fields, but not essential."

Bud Bennett

"Kids are not learning to use the library. They use computers for everything."

Rich Kelly

CHAPTER 5

TESTING—A BIG DEAL ABOUT ABCs AND a + b + c

SAT I... ACT... SAT II... PSAT... PLAN... AP...

THE GRINKLINGS OF ORG

THE MUTANT

S tandardized testing for college starts about the same time the kids hit the wall with adolescent angst. The special tests with all kinds of acronyms, such as SAT, SAT II: Subject Tests, ACT, PLAN, PSAT, and AP, require special planning. Here are some tips on figuring out the acronyms, organization, test prep courses, and broadcasting scores. Some really good news: You don't have to take a test at the end of this chapter.

TEST TAKING—TO PREPARE OR NOT TO PREPARE IS *NOT* THE QUESTION

VOICES OF EXPERIENCE

"Our son hadn't done as well as he wanted to on the SAT the first time he took it. So over the summer he did a lot of self-study, especially with the vocabulary part. The family would be driving somewhere, like to the beach or on a long car trip—and he would have us quiz him from his flash cards. By the end of the summer, his younger sister knew all the vocabulary! The next time he took the test, he raised his score by 250 points."

Joyce Batipps

"I put out every book we had on test preparation, and I ended up putting them away. Our kids wouldn't open them. We also went through private tutors, but what worked was enrolling them in a test prep program where they practiced taking the tests with the instructor present. I don't know any child who will sit down for nine hours a week by himself and study for these tests. Not in America."

Michael Merlin

Taking practice runs with any college entrance exam will not guarantee a perfect score, but it will help your student feel more prepared when the real thing comes along.

People from different regions of the country put more or less emphasis on taking test prep classes. Don't mortgage the farm so your student can enroll in test prep classes. On the other hand, don't totally ignore a chance to prepare for the test, either.

Believe it or not, some students now take test prep courses for the PSAT and again for the SAT. Oh, the insanity of it all.

High school guidance offices have books with practice tests. Bookstores sell how-to books and computer programs with practice tests. You can get them via the Internet. The problem isn't finding practice tests. The problem is setting aside time every day to practice the practice tests. Kind of like those old piano lessons in grade school.

Some high schools provide opportunities for students to learn more about the exams and practice taking them. They learn test-winning skills such as how to prepare differently for essay and multiple-choice questions. Now wouldn't it be a shame to pass that up?

There are also big-name and no-name commercial test preparation classes that stretch over a number of weeks. That's commercial, as in *for-profit*. Investigate the presenters' credentials before you pay the (usually) big bucks. But remember, no company promises Ivy League admission scores in return.

A private tutor is another option. The one-on-one status enables the tutor to determine your child's specific weak areas and show him techniques to cope with those areas. That is obviously helpful, but there are those $$$ signs again.

Sometimes it seems as if everyone says students must take at least one test prep class to succeed. Not true. Whether for economic reasons or their child's preference, lots of people opt for the go-it-alone test prep route.

Some do-it-yourselfers don't bother taking any timed practice tests at home; they go into the test cold and unsuspecting of what's ahead for the next two hours. We don't know why they do that, and we wish they wouldn't.

A golden piece of advice for those students: At the very least, reading directions before test day tells the test taker whether a wrong "guess" answer will hurt the score.

PLAN AND PSAT

Students also may practice under real conditions by taking the PLAN in the sophomore year. PLAN is practice for the ACT. There is also the Practice SAT/National Merit Scholarship Qualifying Test, or PSAT/NMSQT, which students can take in the sophomore and junior years to practice for the SAT (see SAT/ACT and Other Alphabet Tests on page 97).

Each PLAN and PSAT test costs about the same as a movie ticket, so why not sign the kids up and let them practice under real conditions? Then they know exactly what it's like when they take the tests that count in the junior and senior years.

Here's something that gets by a lot of students and parents: Youngsters who want to be eligible to compete for National Merit Scholarships—always a lot of prestige but not always a lot of money—*must* take the PSAT/NMSQT in the fall of the junior year. That's another reason to take the PSAT in the sophomore year. Kind of crazy to have to practice for the practice test, isn't it!

REGISTERING FOR EXAMS

Of course, long before any test day arrives, have your youngster bring home the packets for the PSAT, PLAN, SAT, and ACT from the guidance office. You'll note, and we hope your youngster will note, that there is a deadline for filling out each registration form and sending it in along with your check. Unless your child is unusual, you may have to remind him (more than once!) to complete the registration form.

Your youngster also can register on-line. Check out the details, get out the credit card, and register at *www.collegeboard.org* for the SAT and at *www.act.org* for the ACT.

Suggest your youngster create a separate slot for each test in a brand new accordion file. Keep each test information packet, registration copy, and results together. Then, on a master list at the front of the file, note the test name, date taken, score, and colleges designated to receive the score report. Your student will thank you (mentally, anyway) as she refers to that list every time she fills out a college application.

For the procrastinators of the world, who, most likely, did not follow your accordion file suggestion, late registration costs extra.

You must register by snail mail if you have special circumstances such as:

—being eligible for a fee waiver;
—being unable to take Saturday tests because of religious observances;
—testing closer to home when you live more than 75 miles from the nearest test center;
—missing the late registration deadline and attempting to take the test as a standby, which you can do if there is room after all preregistered students have been admitted;
—special accommodations for students with disabilities.

NOW HEAR THIS: If youngsters want to apply to one of the United States service academies such as the Naval Academy or the Air Force Academy, they should take the standardized tests in the junior year (see "Yes, Sir! I Want to Go to a Service Academy, Sir!" on page 50).

SAT II: SUBJECT TESTS

Back in the Dark Ages Before Parenthood (DABP), we all took something called Achievement Tests that covered what we (maybe) knew in such subjects as math, science, history, or English. Today, those tests are called the SAT II: Subject Tests for English, history, math, sciences, and foreign languages. Some colleges require specific subject tests.

Psst. Test tip for SAT II: Your youngster doesn't need to take all of them on the same day. In fact, taking three tests the same day probably would be to his disadvantage, something like running three long races on the same day. Instead, your student should time taking SAT II tests for the end of the semester when he knows the most about the subject and it's fresh in his mind. Still, practice tests for knowing directions, timing, and question types are in order.

Some youngsters don't take tests well. What's a parent to do? Talk about it together, check with the school counselor, learn test-taking strategies, and practice, practice, practice. If the child has tested consistently poorly through the years and yet maintained a good GPA, point out the GPA record in college interviews and/or application essays.

Just when you thought you'd never win the parent-of-the-year award, a golden opportunity comes along: Tell your child that if he does his best and is satisfied with the test results, you'll be satisfied, too!

"Whether I should pay for test preparation help was never a 'Will I or will I not' issue. It was more like, 'When is the money due?' For me as a mother, there was no choice."

Vivian Brown

TEST STRESS—NOT A PRETTY SIGHT

"I think I was under more stress as the parent than my children were when it came time for them to take the SATs. I wanted them to get good, high scores. So I'd say, 'I don't understand why you aren't in bed now! You have a test in the morning!' They were fine but I wasn't."

Daniel Lazzaro

"We took our son out for breakfast the morning of his ACT test. We wished him luck in the diner parking lot and waved good-bye as he pulled out in his car. He turned his head to wave back, crashed into three cars, and totaled his own car. We left his father there to deal with the aftermath while I drove him to the test site. We arrived on time, but he was obviously upset and his test score reflected that. Because he had already been admitted to the University of Iowa and wanted to go there, he did not retake the test later."

Rickie Pashler

Chapter 5: TESTING—A BIG DEAL ABOUT ABCs AND a + b + c

Test stress can come from so many places that educators and psychiatrists write books about it! "Bad" stress, the kind that hurts performance, may rear its ugly head for any number of reasons, rational or not.

A few stressful scenarios: Maybe the student has a history of weak test scores; wants to achieve a specific score to be within a specific college's range; aims to achieve as highly or higher than some other kids in the class; thinks low scores mean he is stupid and shouldn't or can't go to college; or hopes to please spoken or imagined parental expectations.

Kids also put pressure on each other, whether they realize it or not. Asking a classmate, "Where do you want to go to college?" before she's taken the SAT or ACT can put the student in a tailspin. After all, those test results have to match up with the requirements of her college choices. Otherwise, she'll need to choose other colleges.

If parents have any concern about their student's stress level, they should check with a professional.

Generally, though, test stress might be combated in a number of ways, including:

1. Getting adequate sleep and eating real food instead of junk food.
2. Establishing a routine for preparing for the test(s).
3. Not taking on any new commitments for a while.
4. Lightening up on other responsibilities until the test is over.
5. Reading "Calvin & Hobbes" cartoon books for a laugh a day.
6. Discussing concerns with teachers and/or guidance counselors.

Sometimes, real empathy helps, too. If you took college entrance tests 20 or 25 years ago, can you still remember the terror you felt walking into the exam room? If you do, you can mean it when you put your arm around your youngster and say, "Son, I know how you feel." Actually, your student might find some consolation in that.

Test stress may be the good kind, though, if your student has practiced for the big day. A few butterflies is pretty common. In fact, like an athlete or actor, good stress may help someone who has prepared fully to reach peak performance.

Actually, many students don't seem to register much at all on the test stress scale. Maybe that's because the parents are worrying enough for the whole family.

Or, the students figure that if they don't do well one time, they will be able to take the test again. (This is not true forever and ever.)

After each test score is returned, whatever the score, treat your student honestly and respectfully. That means not overpraising or overmourning. It is, after all, only one score and the sun will come up tomorrow.

> "During senior year, students are busy putting together the yearbook. Ours lists where the seniors plan to go to college after graduation. Things like that can put pressure on a kid when it's time to take tests."
>
> **Jim Evans**

WHAHDJURKIDSCORE?—NO BILLBOARDS PLEASE!

> "Our son went to college in 1990 when affirmative action was in full swing. He said his white fellow classmates assumed he'd gotten into this 'top 25' school because he was black and part of a quota. He wanted to wear his good test scores on his chest, but, of course, he didn't."
>
> **Joyce Batipps**

Once the results are released, the students seem to know immediately what everybody else got. They especially know who did really well among those who are topnotch students to begin with. And *everybody* knows it if somebody nabs a 1600 on the SAT or 36 on the ACT.

However, generally speaking, this who-scored-what information isn't a big deal to the kids.

Parents sharing test results is another matter, one that gets all caught up socially. You don't share with other people how much you earn, or how much your family spent on vacation. And you probably shouldn't share test scores either.

Most kids would rather die than have parents share test scores across the backyard fence. They consider it bragging. After all, if the scores were low, would the parents be chattering away?

The fact is, most students score about where they thought they would. Some will do a little better, others a little worse. If the results indicate your youngster can be admitted to the colleges in which he's interested, the anxiety disappears. (You'll love that part.)

Be prepared to talk with your youngster if she has an older sibling who scored higher. Let her know that she isn't in competition with anyone else, that you're proud of her, and that you love her. Then say it all again, over a pizza of her choice.

"I'd share test results if the issue naturally came up in conversation. But that was never anything that did come up with my friends and me. I can't imagine sitting around and talking about numbers."

Vivian Brown

SAT/ACT AND OTHER ALPHABET TESTS

SAT I, SAT II, PSAT, ACT, PLAN—whoa, that's one mess of acronyms that make up the alphabet soup of standardized tests students usually must take for college admissions. Along with understanding the acronyms, parents need to know what the tests are for and when kids should take the tests. Timing is important for the best results and for meeting application deadlines. Students must register about four weeks before each test, but late registration for an extra fee is possible. Test fees sure can mount up without planning.

Some kids almost become professional SAT test takers, starting in sixth or seventh grade to qualify for special summer academic programs on college campuses. It's not unheard of for high school kids to retake the SAT and ACT two, three, four, even five times (with fresh fees each time) to achieve specific scores either for personal satisfaction or to achieve the score range of a particular college. Of course, that specific score isn't guaranteed, no matter how many times a student fills in those bubble answer sheets. In fact, a score can be lower. For the SAT I, where all test date scores are reported to colleges the student designates, that might not help an application. ACT scores, on the other hand, can be selectively reported by designating a specific test date score. Still, you'll need to check your high school's rules for reporting test scores because they may differ from the SAT and ACT companies' policies.

A whole test industry has evolved to manufacture tests and to teach kids how to "beat" the tests. The Princeton Review and Kaplan are the biggest, best-known, and among the priciest test preparation companies. Rather than teach substantive math or English, they coach students to understand the types of questions and answer choices the test makers write. They also teach test strategy, such as whether it's to your advantage to guess or leave the answer blank if you don't know it. That information is also in the free SAT and ACT packets available on-line or in guidance offices.

Here's a short guide to get you started spooning through the test soup.

- **SAT I**—Scholastic Assessment Test (*www.collegeboard.org*), a three-hour test, mostly multiple choice, to measure verbal and mathematical reasoning. Scores on each subject range from 200 to 800, and generally, schools look at the combined total. Scores are available by telephone (additional $10 fee; credit card required) and by standard mail (no additional fee), usually about four weeks after the test. The test is given seven times from October through June. Students may take the test as many times as they want, but they must reregister ($23.50 fee) each time. Scores are reported to colleges the student designates on the test registration form. Students may request later, for another fee, that scores be sent to additional colleges.

- **SAT II: Subject Tests**—One-hour tests, primarily multiple choice, to measure what the student knows and can apply in one area: writing, literature, math (two levels), biology, chemistry, physics, American history and social studies, world history, reading only in French, German, Italian, Spanish, Latin, and Modern Hebrew, and tests with listening in Chinese, French, German, Japanese, Korean, Spanish, and English Language Proficiency. There are seven test dates but not all subject tests are given on all dates. Students may take up to three subject tests on one test date ($13 basic fee; individual subjects $6 to $11 each). Students may not take the SAT I and SAT II on the same date. Like the SAT I, scores range from 200 to 800. Under a Score Choice program, SAT II scores may be held until the student sees them and requests their release. Once released, though, the scores can't be placed back on hold. Many colleges require one or more specific subject tests for admission, so parents and students need to check prospective colleges before registering for tests.

- **PSAT/NMSQT**—Preliminary SAT/National Merit Scholarship Qualifying Test (*www.collegeboard.org*). The PSAT is administered by high schools in the fall ($9 fee) with score reports generally available to students after Thanksgiving. The test has two purposes: First, it's the gatekeeper for a chance to become a National Merit Scholarship Semifinalist and eligible for a slice of the more than $35 million in tuition aid. Students must take the PSAT in the junior year to be considered. Second, the test taken during sophomore and junior years serves as a (cheap) SAT practice test. As a sidelight, if students sign up for the Student Search Service, they will get tons of mail from colleges.

- ACT—The ACT (*www.act.org*) tests the student's cumulative knowledge and skills in English, math, reading, and science reasoning. Individual scores for each area ranging from 1 to 36 are averaged into a composite score, which is reported to colleges the student designates. Test results are reported four to seven weeks after the test date. Like the SAT, registration is required about four weeks before the test date ($22 fee). Tests are given six times during the school year. Most colleges accept either the ACT or the SAT. Check each school's admissions requirements.

- PLAN—A practice ACT that tests English, math, reading, and science reasoning. The test covers material studied prior to or early in the student's high school career. Students also may participate in an interest inventory for career clues. The test is given each fall in your student's high school ($8 fee). Some schools administer the test to every sophomore; others offer the test on a voluntary basis.

Special accommodations are available for students with diagnosed and documented special needs: visual, hearing, physical, or learning disabilities. Having an IEP, 504 Plan, or professional evaluation does not guarantee eligibility for testing accommodations. Plus, not all test dates are available for all kinds of special needs. Check the information packets and check with the guidance counselor. A request form available from the guidance office must accompany the test registration form. Because of required documentation, students needing accommodations cannot register on-line.

Finally, fees may be waived in some circumstances. Again, talk to the counselor about requirements, and mail the fee-waiver card with the test registration.

CHAPTER 6

CAMPUS VISITS— SLIGHTLY SCARY, AMPLY REWARDING

Campus visits let you test reality versus all those pretty college brochures scattered in your child's bedroom back home. But there's much more than looks to a campus visit: group and one-on-one interviews, tours, sitting in on classes, meeting professors and students, overnights, campus events, and, finally, figuring out what to do afterward. Here are tips to make one of the most fun parts of the college application process a memorable adventure for you and your child.

TIMING'S EVERYTHING—CAMPUS VISITS

VOICES OF EXPERIENCE

"We told our children we would visit as many campuses as possible. But if, in the end, the first pick turned out to be a college we had not visited, we'd definitely go there before making a final decision."

Cyndi Bennett

"We took our son to a loosey-goosey college. The campus was gorgeous, exquisite. They kept saying there were no requirements. He could decide what to study. And dorm life wasn't bad, either. Our college experiences had been more structured so this wasn't very appealing to us. We said, 'Okay, let's look at the literature course offerings.' It was like literature of Nairobi and women's literature of the thirteenth century, compared with a vast, solid curriculum at other schools. We asked him what he thought would be most useful. Even at that point, he could see the difference."

Jane Eckstein

"My wife and I loved Northern Arizona University. She said it looked like summer camp. Our son didn't like the University of Colorado because he said there was too much stuff going on there."

Daniel Lazzaro

One of the biggest changes in the last 20 years in the college search and admissions process is campus visits. In our generation, few students visited colleges. Now, almost everyone thinks they should visit before deciding where they want to spend the next four or five years of their lives.

Campus visits are full of flavor. What does the campus feel like? What do the students look like? Is the cafeteria food really that bad? The best brochure or web site in the world can't compare to touring a campus. Besides, traveling to a campus gives your student a better idea of the distance from home than simply looking at a dot on the map. Dots don't look that far away.

Some high schools offer bus trips to a number of colleges, whirlwind tours meant for winnowing choices. They're exhausting, which is why the kids go and the parents stay home. Your turn comes next, when the list of stops is shorter and the time on campus is longer. (Read your turn as "more sane, less exhausting.")

Visiting a number of campuses exposes your child to the dizzying array of possibilities waiting out there. If you can afford the trips, they are well worth it. But don't even try to go to every college your kid has on The Long, Meandering List of Colleges.

It's best, but not always affordable, to visit only a few campuses per trip. Too many become a blur. If you are doing a bunch in a crunch, plan on no more than two colleges each day. A productive visit takes a minimum of three hours per campus: an hour for the tour, an hour for the group meeting with the admissions representative, an hour for a personal interview. And you still haven't had any real walk-around-alone time.

Your first call should be to the Admissions Office to sign up for the group interview, a personal interview if that's an option, and a campus tour. At the same time, set up any special requests, such as attending a class or meeting with professors or department chairpersons. The office also usually can provide a list of area accommodations and answer questions about timing. This first call is actually a good test of how user-friendly the college will be for your student.

Not-so-good news for procrastinators: If you intend to visit highly selective or "hot" colleges, be aware that if they offer personal interviews, the fall slots are often filled by mid-July, but do call back periodically to see if someone has canceled. One family, who had been told in July that all slots were taken, stopped into the Admissions Office in October just to show the student's serious interest. An admissions representative said he had just received a cancellation and would be happy to visit with the student right then.

WHEN TO VISIT

If you're like most families, you'll visit campuses in the spring of your child's junior year. The problem is, you can't imagine how complicated that spring can be until it actually is that spring. Different things come up, such as events, work, commitments. And fall of the senior year won't be any better. Plan as far ahead as possible!

It ought to be a law—tour the campus when school is in session. If you arrive when the college students are off partying on their spring break, which is what many do, you can't get a "feel" for the place.

If you can include part of one weekend day on the campus, it helps you realize what life will be like when your child isn't in class. If the campus is deserted because everybody went home to do their laundry, but your child will be too far away to go home no matter how dirty the clothes, it may mean some lonely Saturdays and Sundays in the dorm.

Touring campus while summer school is in session isn't the same, especially at smaller colleges. The students probably aren't the same ones who are there during the year, and their numbers are smaller. Also, the pace is slower and there aren't as many big events going on.

If possible, visit favorite campuses several times and at different times of the year. After all, anybody can put on a good show once. Go again the week before college finals, when things are sort of falling apart.

If you're a working parent who can't tour campuses during the high school's spring break, you may need to pull your child out of school to make the trip at another time. Teachers won't like that, but, again, it is important to visit colleges when students are on campus. Know your high school's attendance policy before you plan to take trips on school days. Some schools excuse students for college visits and some don't.

Juniors and seniors in high school can be pretty testy. (Surely you've noticed that!) Visiting colleges with your high schooler can be a surprisingly refreshing experience because you're on neutral ground. It can be a great time to talk. Plus, this is one of very few settings where kids think it's okay to be seen with their parents. (We know you aren't hanging out with them on Saturday nights back home!)

AFTER THE INTERVIEW

Still, campus visits that include personal interviews may not be quite as refreshing an experience, at least not until the interview is over. You can tell your child that meeting with an admissions officer is an "exciting opportunity," but to most kids, it looks scarier than a Freddie Krueger movie.

If, after you have visited your very first college, your child announces that it is the only school she'll ever want to attend, keep traveling. Her decision is premature; she still needs to compare schools.

Don't be surprised if your youngster wants to leave ten minutes after you've arrived at the college he has been proclaiming for months as the school to die for. Kids have a sixth sense that instantly spots things the parents don't see for hours.

"Our daughter wanted to attend a small, state-supported institution away from home. She loved Northwest Missouri State in Maryville but wondered where the mall was (when we visited the campus). When we pointed out Wal-Mart, she wasn't interested any longer. Eventually, she decided on the University of Nebraska at Lincoln, where there's a mall. She joined a sorority to find a smaller community in a bigger school."

Janet Heimbuch

"We knew we couldn't circle around to all the schools our youngster wanted to visit, so we said we'd be glad to take him to whatever schools he was serious about."

Don Polden

"AND TO YOUR LEFT IS THE STUDENT UNION..."

"My daughter and I dressed up a little bit, but we discovered that when you're an art student, you don't really need to do that. We walked into one place in the middle of Manhattan and there was purple hair all over the place. We were the ones who stuck out."

Dianne Peterson

"Our son crossed one college off his list the minute the campus tour was over because the guide made disparaging remarks about college professors. His father is a college professor."

Jane Eckstein

Campus visits without the guided tour aren't worth the effort. But call ahead for dates and times because tours aren't conducted 24-7. They do go on rain, shine, sleet, or snow, however, so dress for the weather and *wear comfortable shoes.*

It's not unusual for prospective students to dress casually when visiting a campus. We know, you wore your Sunday best, or close to it, when you were the kid taking the tour. Today, it's different. Admissions officers realize the prospective students and assorted family members are going from one college to another, so casual's okay. Stylish casual, that is.

For some kids, stylish casual means a tongue stud, eyebrow metal, and 15 or so earrings on one ear. However, that look probably won't work well in an interview at a stuffy college. You have to ask the youngster, "Do you want the interviewer to look at your tongue or listen to your thoughts?"

Campus tour guides can cause a prospective student to sign on the dotted line or flee off campus, never again to utter a kind word about the school. Because of that, campus guides won't always be a reliable indication of the institution. You may have the best guide on the staff at School A and the worst guide on the staff at School B, but that doesn't mean your overall impressions of the two schools will be accurate.

If you're lucky, your tour guide will be a current student. Good student guides are enthusiastic, knowledgeable, and honest about their college. They can give you a valuable firsthand sense of the institution and what to expect. And they are able to walk backward for long periods of time without falling down.

It's great if the guides present a mix of the academic, which *you* want to see, with the social, which *your youngster* wants to see.

You'll see the usual bricks and mortar, but look beyond, too, for these items:

- The condition of the dorm rooms often will make even the most stout-hearted parents cringe. And what's really curious is that it seems the richer the school, the worse the condition of their dorms. Probably those Ivies don't need to put money into amenities to attract students.
- Note the size of those rooms. (Read that as "tiny.") When your child asks, "How can I fit all my things into that room?" point out that at least one other person will also be fitting things into that room.
- Is there a computer lab in the dorm or nearby?
- Will your freshman have a l-o-o-o-ong way to walk from the dorm to classes?
- Are there laundry and kitchen facilities in the freshman dorms?
- Are the campus parking lots filled with ten-year-old Probes or brand new BMWs?

- Is there any new construction? Are old buildings kept up?
- Do you see phones to call campus security? Are the campus and parking lots amply lighted?
- Talk to students sitting around in the student union. (Students sit around, drink coffee, and study a lot.) Ask them if this college was their first choice. What made them come here? Were there any big surprises? What do they wish were different? What do people do on weekends? What about drugs, alcohol, and parties on campus? Students usually give straight answers.
- What's the gym equipment like? How about the science lab equipment?
- What are the meal options and hours?

"Touring campus with our children allowed us to have the dialogue that you don't have at the breakfast table. The tours served as a good subject matter for discussion."

Joyce Batipps

"We arrived at one campus earlier than we'd expected and started looking around. A professor noticed us strangers, came up, introduced himself, and took us into the faculty lounge for breakfast. Then he found a young lady to give us a tour. He made a real impression."

Vivian Brown

"Our son liked the University of California at Davis because there was a farmer's market every Wednesday and Saturday. He knew he was going to hate dorm food and he loves to cook."

Daniel Lazzaro

WHY GO FOR AN INTERVIEW—AND WHY NOT

"I think 'specialty' institutions tend to do more on-campus interviewing than large schools. Specialty schools recruit, almost like a football coach. Our daughter was looking at art schools, and they wanted her to interview. The experience was helpful because she had questions she wanted to ask of them too, about studio space, the dorm situation, and off-campus residences."

Dianne Peterson

"Several schools called my son on the phone, but he didn't have on-campus interviews with those colleges. They already had his essay, which addressed what he had done with his life so far, what he wanted to study, and what goals he had set. They asked him a lot of questions on the phone. It was all very casual."

Audrey Valhuerdi

The thing about an on-campus interview is that it tells your student, "Hey, somebody's interested in me."

Sometimes it comes down to a numbers game. College applications are up, partly because there are more high school graduates than ever, which means selective colleges can be more choosy about whom they admit. Thus, the on-campus interview becomes one more opportunity for your student to etch her name in the admission officer's consciousness.

Some colleges send out a postcard or letter prior to the prospective student's campus visit. The correspondence says, "We hear you'll be here and we would like to meet you" (or something like that). That could mean a full-fledged, one-on-one interview in a carpeted office, or it may mean gathering 30 students and parents together in the admissions reception area for a Q&A session. Know which scenario your youngster will be part of ahead of time.

One-on-one interviews may be for evaluation or for information only. Particularly in smaller colleges, the representatives may have visited with prospective students at their schools or by telephone and have a pretty good feel for the candidate, negating the need for an evaluative interview. But be aware: The reps would need to be unconscious to not naturally notice conduct and language during on-campus chats.

If the colleges you plan to visit conduct optional on-campus interviews, and if you and your child decide to take up that option, have your youngster make an appointment at least four weeks ahead of time.

QUIZ TIME

In most families, telling the youngster what questions to ask in the interview is about as effective as telling him that bedtime's been moved back to 9:00 P.M. Better that you slip in suggestions about what to ask while you're passing the potatoes or washing the dishes or heading to the mall to buy him new jeans.

Better yet, suggest that your youngster draw up a list of questions ahead of time. There's no way your child is going to remember all of the questions bouncing around inside his brain (and parents generally do not sit in on the interview).

Even if your youngster could remember all the questions, there probably wouldn't be enough time to ask them. So make one more suggestion—that the questions be listed in priority order. That way, your youngster may not get around to asking if there are Ping Pong tables on campus, but she will find out whether incoming freshmen are guaranteed a room.

Your child may give higher priority to some questions than you would. For instance, you may not in a hundred years wonder about the school's men-to-women ratio, but that might be your youngster's second question, right behind "Do you have to eat in the cafeteria?"

Gentle reminder: Kids ask questions that are important to them.

Have your student bring a copy of his high school transcript and his updated résumé to the personal interview. Sometimes, students must fill out an information sheet before the interview so all the information will be handy. Plus, it's an easy way to get the conversation started.

It's okay if your youngster takes notes during the interview. Note taking tells the college official that your student is serious about what's being said.

Turnabout is fair play, so your youngster should be prepared to answer questions as well as ask them. Preparation simply means thinking about topics in terms of some concrete examples with "Why?" as the natural followup.

Scripting and memorizing answers to potential questions is a pure waste of time; there are too many possibilities and the student could forget the script in mid-answer and draw a blank. In addition, the student won't sound natural.

Your youngster may be relieved to know that answers should be concise, honest, and conversational. She should make eye contact, smile, and sit up straight—all those things you've been saying all these years are finally useful!

Interviewer questions range from the general—"Tell me about yourself (or family or school)" to the particular—"What unrequired books have you read in the past year?" Other possible topics:

- Why college in general;
- Why this specific college;
- Other colleges on your list;
- Possible major;
- Favorite TV shows, books, authors, magazines, teachers, classes, activities, contributions to school (church, community);

- Heroes and models, living or dead, and how they influence you;
- Achievements, strengths, weaknesses;
- Significant events in your life;
- Self-knowledge: What makes you happy, sad, satisfied, angry; adjectives describing you; work ethic; intellectual curiosity; concerns about college; short- and long-term goals; defining success;
- What you'd like the interviewer to most remember or know about you;
- What you'd add to the college.

If there is a particular program or department chair your child really wants to speak with, have the youngster make that appointment ahead of time, too. This is especially helpful for students who will be in theater, art, music, or an area requiring research. Do only seniors get meaty parts in the play? Are only seniors allowed to do research? Where do those graduates get jobs?

Some colleges even allow visiting high school students to sit in on a class or two.

POSTMORTEMS

After each campus visit, head for a quiet little coffeehouse where you and your youngster can talk about what was positive and negative, exciting and disappointing, important and ridiculous about the college just visited. Suggest that your student jot down some thoughts in a notebook you just happened to bring along.

Why jot now? Because your youngster's impressions of and feelings about the school he just visited are clear in his mind. Another campus or two later, recollections will be more muddy, less clear.

You've probably collected a wheelbarrow full of facts about the college. What needs to be jotted down is less specific: What was there to like and dislike about the campus? Classrooms? Labs? Dorms? Was the atmosphere friendly? Inviting? Stuffy? Stilted? How did the student body look and act? Did your student feel as if she'd fit in there? If that college is still appealing, why?

Rate the tour guide, as well as those who ran any meetings or interviews. Include professors with whom you spoke. All of them reflect, or should reflect, the atmosphere of their college.

It would be great if your youngster seeks your opinion of the college. But tread carefully. Kids this age can switch on the "contrary" button with little or no warning.

IN LIEU OF THE ON-CAMPUS INTERVIEW

In lieu of on-campus interviews, some students receive phone calls from the Admissions Office. It's a good chance to chat, but make sure your youngster keeps his thinking cap on while chatting. This isn't like talking to the neighbor down the street.

If any of the colleges you and your child are visiting don't do on-campus interviews, ask if an admissions rep will be visiting your youngster's high school soon. Meeting and talking with that person may mean the college will take on additional weight in the application process later on.

Instead of an on-campus interview, or perhaps in addition to it, some students are interviewed in their hometown by designated alumni from the area. Interviews take place in an office or neutral public place, such as a restaurant or bookstore. Students should regard the interviews as meaningful as if they were on campus. Parents definitely are *not* invited. Afterward, the interviewer sends an evaluation report to the college.

VOICES OF EXPERIENCE

"Our daughter really liked one particular school, but she thought the interviewer asked some strange questions, such as, 'You can only hurt yourself by being in this interview. Why are you here?' and 'Tell me about your boyfriend.' She said everybody else on campus was terrific. We thought perhaps he represented an institutional administrative philosophy that was not friendly to women, and after much agonizing, told her we could not financially support her at that institution."

Jim Adams

"During our son's interview, they asked him about current events, his favorite books, what he was interested in, whether he did any community service. He told them he was going to go to the Dominican Republic for three weeks. He was so nonchalant about the whole thing."

Jennifer Merlin

"My son had three interviews. One was as part of a group, two were one-on-one, and one of those was with an upper classman. He would never come to me and say, 'Mom, what should I ask during my interview?' He felt that if he couldn't handle the interviews, how could he handle a college."

Gail Walzer

PARENTS HAVE QUESTIONS, TOO!

VOICES OF EXPERIENCE

"I don't know as you can actually prepare questions. Ours were more impromptu questions brought on by what we were seeing on the campus tour. For example, my daughter asked what was there to do in the city, and the guide said everything was here on campus. Students never had to leave the campus for entertainment. His response was helpful because it served as a definite turnoff for our daughter, a kid who loved exploring cities for what they had to offer."

Joyce Batipps

If your youngster has a one-on-one interview, you'll probably not be present. If, on the other hand, the admissions officer meets with your whole tour group, questions may come from both prospective students and parents. Know that when you are the one asking a question, your child will be grimacing. Remember, high schoolers don't think parents are all that bright.

Or, if your tour group splits up, with the students going in one direction and the adults in another, you can ask lots of questions without embarrassing your youngster.

Whatever the situation, if you have questions, ask them. Choosing a particular college is far too important for a high school student to handle alone. And besides, in most cases, who will be paying the bills?

There are other ways to gather information on your own, as well:

1. Try to find a student newspaper and/or magazine to scan or take home. You'll get an unvarnished student view of campus life and business.
2. Observe other parents and applicants in the reception area for a quick snapshot of types of prospective students interested in the school.
3. Talk to any student ambassadors hanging around. See what they are like as individuals and ask their insights into college life.
4. Go outside and watch students. Do they hurry, tarry, converse, laugh, mingle? Or do they look hunkered down, alone, scurrying like moles to libraries or classes? Think about what your child might prefer.
5. Engage a professor in conversation. Ask about the academic prowess of students, their intellectual curiosity level, how they prepare for class. Do

students like to learn generally? How many students does the professor know by name?

6. Note office hours on professors' doors to gauge accessibility.

7. Visit the campus art museum.

8. Visit the library—your student surely won't! Are there ample study carrels? Comfortable chairs? Lighting? Table space? Staff? Are students socializing or studying? Are there foreign-language and English magazines and newspapers?

Sometimes the admissions representative will chat briefly with parents following the student's interview. It's not the time to tell about the 60,000 lives your youngster saved on the way to school one day. Nor is it the time to roll your eyes about what a procrastinator and disorganized teenager she is (see Questions—What Was I Going to Ask? at the end of this chapter).

If you are lucky, the same representative will visit your home area and you'll be able to connect again. Kids disdain such connections, but they help the representative get a better picture of the prospective student, convincing the rep to advocate for the student's admission.

"There are so many options for getting through college. I sat in on a discussion about the five-year plan. A kid would never sit in on a discussion about that."

Dianne Peterson

"Our HMO doesn't cover the county where our child is going to school. Our kid would never think to ask about that."

Michael Merlin

BETTER EYE-OPENERS THAN CLASSES—OVERNIGHTS

"Our daughter nixed an East Coast, big city school because the young woman she stayed overnight with during her campus visit was snooty. We thought that was curious, since the young woman came from a small midwestern city, just like we did! Anyway, we nixed the school, too, but we did it because there were bars on all the first floor windows."

Dennis Rhodes

> "I wish all colleges would let all prospective students spend the night on campus. That's when you really meet the college students."
>
> Kathy Hafner

This is the time to find out whether the promises of a dorm filled with exercise facilities and a cafeteria filled with healthful foods really are just empty promises.

The schools where your child decides to spend overnights are probably the schools that will end up in the final selection batch. That's because staying overnight is a big commitment, and often an uncomfortable thing to do because your youngster is with a bunch of strangers.

Those overnights aren't like pulling into a motel at 5:00 P.M. to see if there's a room available. Your youngster needs to arrange the stay with the Admissions Office well ahead of time. Generally, students host prospectives, taking them to dinner at the dining hall and introducing them to other students.

Obviously, staying overnight on campus with an older friend makes the experience easier, and probably just as valid.

Colleges also have special visitation days or weekends for prospective students. Plans will include anything from tickets to a sporting or fine arts event to meetings with deans, professors, and students. It's a fun time for a group of prospectives to exchange information on other colleges. And they get fed, always paramount at that age.

Often, colleges offer special visits or overnights for accepted students. If at all possible, the student should go, meet the people who might be classmates, and check out the school once more before accepting the acceptance. If your student comes home wearing a baseball cap or sweatshirt emblazoned with the college name, that probably means a big "Yes!"

VOICES OF EXPERIENCE

> "Our son wanted to go to Wisconsin for years. Then he spent a weekend on campus and realized that when the snows came, there was no way he was going to get up every morning and walk who-knows-where to class. I was amazed because that school was all he had thought about. So some maturity came through."
>
> Wally Gingerich

BACK HOME AGAIN—
THE CONVERSATION CONTINUES

VOICES OF EXPERIENCE

"I got the feeling that the more I liked something, the less my daughter liked it. She probably thought there must be something wrong with a particular school if your parents want you to go there. I knew she was making up her mind so I didn't say anything one way or the other about how I felt personally."

Kathy Hafner

Who appreciates thank-you notes? Probably admissions officers, especially those who grant personal interviews, and professors who gave of their time to talk with prospective students.

If your youngster is so inclined, now is the time to talk things over. But don't be surprised if your student has formed instant impressions of certain colleges based on unscientific observations such as:

- I liked School A because the kids all wore khakis.
- I didn't like School B because there were hardly any trees on campus.
- I liked School C because the gumbo we had in the cafeteria was great.
- I didn't like School D because the gumbo we had in the cafeteria was gross. (A student should not choose a school based on gumbo.)
- I liked School E because it's close to home so I can still do my laundry when I come home on the weekends.
- I didn't like School F because every single kid on that campus was stuck up. (Probably that is not the case.)

To your child, one campus is cool; another is disgusting. This may not be how you see either campus, but who is going to be living there? Once the kid determines a particular college is disgusting, you might as well eliminate that possibility.

Ask probing questions: How did you like the campus? How did you feel there?

As you discuss the pros and cons of each campus visited, listen to your child's impressions instead of announcing what you think. For lots of parents, this is as tough as chewing nails, although much more productive.

Still, some issues demand your comment. For example, what if one of the colleges being considered offers only independent study, and your child is motivated by deadlines and rules imposed by others? If a situation is not acceptable, that needs to become part of the conversation now.

What you're doing, whether you know it or not, is moving from The Long, Meandering List of Colleges toward The Short, Pretty Serious List of Colleges (see Chapter 7).

Begin that move by filling in any remaining information holes. If you or your youngster still have questions that weren't answered during the campus visits, call colleges back and get the answers.

Some colleges provide high schoolers with contact names of on-campus students who will address those leftover questions.

If possible, help your child make arrangements to talk with a graduate of each school visited. You can get names from web sites or the alumni or administration offices.

VOICES OF EXPERIENCE

"We'd talk about colleges in general. I'd ask my kids what was important to them. Then I'd use those points as a basis for discussion after visiting a college."

Diane Lenahan

QUESTIONS—WHAT ARE THEY GOING TO ASK?

Anticipating what questions admissions officers may ask will help your student prepare for a one-on-one interview. Obviously, the interviewer will ask basic questions—about grades, extracurricular activities, athletics, community service, and so on. But a good interviewer also will ask questions that go beyond the facts, questions that require some thought and maturity to answer well. For example:

- What are your special attributes?
- What are your biggest accomplishments?
- What's been your biggest disappointment? How did you handle it?
- Do you perceive yourself as a leader? Why?

- Do you perceive yourself as a creative person?
- Do you see yourself as being intellectually curious? Can you give an example?
- Would you describe yourself as a responsible person? Why?
- What motivates you?
- What are your goals? How were they set? How are they measured?
- Describe your sense of humor.
- What can you contribute to our college community?
- Are there special circumstances in your life that our school needs to know about?
- What makes you different from the other students applying to our institution? Why should we admit you over someone else?
- What is important to you?

QUESTIONS—WHAT WAS I GOING TO ASK?

Don't just drink in the information admissions officers provide. Ask questions about:

- **FRESHMEN.** When do students declare a major? What percent of students do not return sophomore year? What services do you offer students who need help adjusting to being away from home?

- **TECHNOLOGY.** What kind of computer will my youngster need? Are the dorms wired for the Internet? Are hookups free? Can you take notes on computer in classes? Are students allowed or required to write tests on a computer?

- **COSTS.** What is the *actual* cost of sending my child to your institution? What if my financial situation changes and I have problems paying your bills? How and when do I qualify for financial aid?

- **SCHOLARSHIPS.** How does my child apply for scholarships? Does this mean the college's scholarships or in general? Merit or need-based? Are scholarships renewable for all four years?

- **CLASSES.** How many freshman courses are taught by graduate students? What is your average class size? How do you award Advanced Placement credit? How do you determine eligibility for the honors program? Will I get a copy of my child's grades?

- **FACULTY.** How does the advising system work? How many teachers will be on sabbatical at the same time?

- **HOUSING.** How easy—or hard—is it to get a room in one of the residence halls? Do certain dorms have certain lifestyles?

- **HEALTH CARE.** What about medical care if my child gets sick? Does the school provide medical insurance, or will the family medical insurance be valid when my child is living on a campus? Will my child have to pay the doctor up front, then be reimbursed?

- **SAFETY.** What provisions are in place for building security and walking on campus at night?

- **GRADUATION.** How easy is it—or more realistically, how *hard* is it—to earn a degree in four years? In five or six years? What if my child changes majors?

- **BEYOND GRADUATION.** How easy is it to get a job after graduation? (Now, why would a parent ask that?) What percentage of students goes on to graduate or professional school?

CHAPTER 7

FILLING OUT FORMS—THE ROAD TO THE "FINAL FOUR" COLLEGE PICKS

At first, you think this part will be easy. Then you discover your youngster is too busy to fill out the applications, not to mention writing the essays. Here's how to reduce The Long, Meandering List of Colleges into The Short, Pretty Serious List of Colleges, and then how to deal with all those forms and procrastinating children.

A CHART AND A PRAYER—MAKING CHOICES

VOICES OF EXPERIENCE

"You are trying to make such mature, life-changing decisions with your child. But high school students are not mature. They're still kids, self-absorbed and without the capacity or ability to make decisions on their own about where they're going to go to college."

Don Polden

"I grew up in segregated schools but my self-esteem was never an issue because the people around me understood what I needed. When our children were in elementary school, this was not the case. Therefore, we had to pump them up before they left home because before the day ended, something would happen to make them question their self-worth. They were not exposed to minority teachers in any significant way. We decided they would attend a historically black college as undergrads to get the nurturing they needed."

Eunice Harris

Going through the college selection process with the first child is tough, partly because you're learning right along with your student. But then, isn't that what you've been doing ever since the kid was born?

Talk now about the fact that you will have input into the final decision. How much? Good question. It's *your* kid and, most likely, *your* money but overinvolvement can become a source of conflict. Together, you and your child must discuss guidelines and specific tasks for each other. The list of colleges to which applications will be sent is too important for a child to draw up alone.

Revisit those parameters you set (you did, didn't you?) for building The Long, Meandering List of Colleges (see Chapter 2). What's more important now—size, housing, religious affiliation, environment, or what? You'll need to rethink and narrow your priorities.

Go back to the school guidance counselor if questions have popped up since you first set parameters. Then have your student gather up the printed materials handed out during the campus tours, the copious notes taken during the on-campus interview and afterward (we hope your youngster can still find those copious notes), the literature each school provided, The Long, Meandering List of Colleges, and everything in those big accordion files.

Review the information you've collected about schools in the "not visited but still considered" pile. Also, if additional schools have caught your eye, or your student's eye, since you put together The Long, Meandering List of Colleges, gather as much information as possible about them now. Realize, however, that the scales probably will tip in favor of schools visited.

THE SHORT, PRETTY SERIOUS LIST OF COLLEGES

Now, with all of that research at your fingertips, you and your child can begin putting together The Short, Pretty Serious List of Colleges (see Appendices, on page 207).

Once The Short, Pretty Serious List of Colleges is started (sometimes, starting requires Herculean effort), discussions take on a more serious tone. Be prepared, though, for out-of-nowhere irrationality. For instance, what if your youngster announces, "I want to go to Pepperdine because I just love the name!" or "I have to go to Bennington because it's so quaint and so New England!" It happens! We suggest you say No, give your reasons, and wait for the kid to get over the hissy fit that is guaranteed to occur.

What if your daughter's boyfriend is going to College A so your daughter believes she must be there, too, even though College A is not suited to her? Or, what if your son's girlfriend is going to College B so your son . . . well, you get the picture. See the suggestion in the previous tip, noting that this time, the hissy fit may be louder and last longer.

Listen to what your child likes or doesn't like about each college. But don't try to pin your student down about why because he probably won't know. You need to trust that your student will know what feels right. In fact, there may be two or three schools that get on The Short, Pretty Serious List of Colleges because they "feel right."

Step back and take an honest look at your child. Consider needs, wants, and abilities. For example, if your child lacks maturity or confidence, small colleges often provide a lot of support for such youngsters, which keeps them going until they mature. Large universities also provide support, but students often must be more proactive in seeking it.

Consider, too, that just because your child may have prospered academically, socially, and activity-wise in high school doesn't mean she will be okay no matter which college is chosen. Part of a good college match comes down to the personality of both the school and the youngster.

You've probably figured out already that a bad match can be costly to you and devastating for your child. That's why the size and location of the school, its atmosphere, and the programs offered must be matched against your child's personality and needs.

Realize that each of your children is different. The way one child compiled a list of colleges may not be the best way for the next sibling to do it.

Allow siblings with different personalities to go to different colleges if they wish. Being the little brother or the kid sister on campus can be tough. Besides, sometimes the only thing siblings have in common are their parents.

"In the weeding out process, my son decided he didn't want to go to one college because of coed dorms and excessive alcohol. On his campus visit, he saw towers built from beer cans in the rooms. The whole thing to him seemed to be like living in a noisy hotel."

Paula Dawson

"Our boys, who were one year apart, were in sports. They got a lot of calls from coaches, and it became confusing because there were so many different sales pitches from the colleges. While the boys were complimented by each call they received, we did feel that we needed to guide them. We knew their futures would be affected by what was happening right now. We told them to pick three schools and look at the academics. They were going for education, Christian values, and then the coach. In that order."

Diana Pace

WHATAYAWANNA MAJOR IN?

"We know one family who wouldn't let their children major in anything as nebulous as English literature. They'd say, 'What kind of job can the kid get with a major like that?' They didn't see the value of learning for the sake of learning. Their kids majored in rigid disciplines like business and engineering so they could get jobs. Period."

Dennis Rhodes

"There is so much pressure for educators to present all the career options to kids so they'll know what they want do when they leave high school. 'What do you want to do?' is coming way too early from everybody. Kids just need to know the options that are out there."

Nancy Johnson

In a nutshell, parents disagree on how kids should pick majors. Some say: College is more than preparation for a job. College is an opportunity to learn how to think, to be able to change careers without retraining. Others say: For all the money college will cost, the least you can expect is that the graduate will come away with career skills that will land her a job before the ink on her diploma is dry.

Regardless of your philosophy, don't automatically expect your child to know what he wants to study. Most don't at this point, and those who do probably won't tell you anyway.

Trade schools, community colleges, or professionally oriented programs within universities are geared toward jobs and specific careers. That's their purpose and in most instances, they fulfill that purpose well. Liberal arts curriculums, on the other hand, stress knowledge in a number of areas with a concentration or major in one or two areas. Liberal arts career choices range from investment banker in New York City to licensed fishing guide in Montana.

An enthusiastic teacher may unwittingly urge a student to pursue that teacher's passion without recognizing what the kid's passion is. Your child needs to concentrate on personal likes as opposed to what a favorite teacher likes.

Some students can be good at almost anything. Let's say your daughter is interested in law, medicine, and the stage. So you spend hours visualizing her hanging an attorney-at-law or an M.D. shingle outside her door. Meanwhile, she's visualizing a star!

Then there are those students who can be good at almost anything, but can't seem to decide *what* they want hanging outside their door.

What's a parent to do? Any number of things, some or all of which might work, including:

1. Direct your student's thought process by asking: Why are we sending you to college? What kinds of jobs and careers do philosophy, English literature, great religions of the world, or (fill-in-the-blank) majors have? Expect the youngster not to know the answers and that's okay. Your point is to get the student to think.

2. When your youngster keeps getting asked, "Whaddayawannado?" or "Whaddayagonna major in?" and she is clueless, send her to the high school guidance office to use the computer programs for interests in careers. Of course, the results may tell your teenager who floats from one thing to another that she should be an actuary. Still, the options may lead to something.

3. Encourage consideration of a double major if your student's passion is not in an obviously marketable field. Talk about keeping as many options open as possible and figuring out a Plan B, in case it's needed sometime.

4. Arrange for your youngster to speak with people who have careers in your child's area of interest. They can discuss how they got where they are today and if they are happy with their work.

5. Back to the library and bookstore for you and, maybe, your youngster, who's pretty busy with school and all this college application stuff. Bring home books about jobs and careers in fields your student considers his calling right now.

6. And speaking of right now, your child may say, "I'm going to be an engineer and I will never, *ever* change my mind." But a year or two into college, he may call home and say, "I don't want to be an engineer anymore." Wow! How human! (A little expensive, maybe, but human.) What he will need at that point, are supportive parents.

What can we say about the student who decides to major in biology because there isn't a language requirement?! (We did *not* make this up.)

Some youngsters confronted with "Whaddayawanna study next year?" may begin saying, "I don't really know about going to college next year. Maybe I'll wait a year." Generally, that hesitation will rectify itself, but for a few students, waiting a year won't be the worst thing that could happen. Depending upon the individual, it may be the *best* thing that could happen.

VOICES OF EXPERIENCE

"Our daughter knew in grade school that she wanted to be a veterinarian. She chose her undergraduate school by where it was ranked as far as acceptance of graduates to vet schools later on."

Rose Kelly

"The aptitude test helped our daughter. It indicated her interest was in interior design, which is her focus. It suggested the area of architecture for our son, this boy whom we couldn't even convince to take a drafting class. But I will say, you should see his Legos!"

Nancy Johnson

MORE ART THAN SCIENCE—HOW TO APPLY

VOICES OF EXPERIENCE

"My son filled out the application papers by himself, but my daughter had no clue about what was going on during her own application process. I ended up filling out the papers for her. Later, when she said she wanted to study abroad, I asked her how many days she would be gone and how much it would cost. She had no clue. This time, I made her be involved so she would finally know the hours I'd spent on those initial college applications."

Sheila Ayala

"Our oldest decided to apply to a college that didn't require an essay. We said that was okay, but told him he would also need to apply to two colleges that required essays. We wanted him to have that writing experience."

Rose Kelly

Think of applications as a shared responsibility; ask your youngster how you can help. If he replies, "Thanks, but I don't need your help. I'll get it done," smile, honor his request, and go learn to play the bagpipes.

Applications usually cost somewhere between $20 and $50 apiece. But not always. For example, some colleges have waived the application fee if prospectives visit campus within a certain time frame, if the student is the child of an alum, or if the student applies electronically.

The expense of multiple applications, plus the time required to fill out a different form for each college used to mean students applied to only a handful of schools. Free electronic applications are changing that.

Web sites for information and on-line applications have proliferated like guppies in a fishbowl. Electronic applications mean students can apply without the knowledge of or assistance from a parent or a counselor. But that doesn't mean the colleges they select will be the best ones for them. It's still important for students to apply to colleges that will represent a good match.

RULE OF TWOS

Because it's still quality, not quantity, that counts, consider the Rule of Twos: Apply to two "safe" schools, two "maybe" schools, and two "reach" colleges. If your student wants to apply to 15 schools, you have to wonder if he missed that step in the process where we talked about setting parameters.

- A "safe" school is one where admission is almost automatic. For instance, some schools accept most qualified applicants. And some state schools guarantee admittance if students score at or above a certain level on the SAT or ACT or fall within, say, the top half of their graduating class. Safe schools should be ones your student actually will want to attend. It's no good if the acceptance letter comes and she says, "So what?! I won't go there in a million years!"

- A "maybe" school isn't a sure thing, but your student and the school's requirements match up pretty well. It probably helps, too, if the school isn't swamped with applicants from your area or high school.

- "Reach" schools vary with each applicant's abilities. Ivy League schools are "reach" schools for just about everyone, and the numbers prove it: An Ivy may have 17,000 applicants for 1,600 spots! In fact, Ivies are so iffy that almost no one should count on them for acceptance. The trick for you as a parent is to convince your kid that even with a 1500 SAT, he still should apply to several schools of varying difficulty for getting in, not just the Ivy of his choice. Schools like Princeton simply cannot take 14,000 freshmen, no matter how qualified each one is (and they are all pretty much superqualified).

ADMISSION—WHEN?

Even though admission seems at least 100 years down the road, your student needs to know that there are about as many kinds of admittance as M&M colors. There is:

- **REGULAR ADMISSION.** A school notifies students about acceptance or rejection in April.

- **ROLLING ADMISSION.** A school notifies students as soon as it has reviewed applications. This is becoming increasingly popular.

- **EARLY DECISION.** A school notifies students in December. If accepted, they must attend that college, as agreed on the application.

- **EARLY ACTION.** Again, the school notifies students in December, but if accepted, they need not commit until the standard May date for regular admissions.

Wait, there's more! Some institutions offer early-early decision, accepting students during their high school junior year, and they're not athletes! And some schools have early decision II for January applications, where seniors get a quick answer and acceptance is binding.

Each institution sets its early decision and action rules, meaning the rules can change each year if the school is so inclined. If you have any questions after reading the school's current literature, be sure to call the admissions representative.

Some arguments for going early decision:

- Like the early bird, an early decision applicant beats the crowd and has less competition for acceptance. That's because some schools give up to half—some give even more!—of their freshman slots to early decision or early action students. If your student decides not to go for early decision, there will be fewer slots available come spring.

- If your kid goes early decision, you and he avoid the nail biting while waiting for the April notification that comes with regular admission, although you may not have to wait that long if the school uses rolling admission. Wonderful as that may be, however, it is not a stand-alone reason for going the early decision route.

Some arguments for not going early decision:

- Early decision assumes students are mature enough to know which college is best for them by the fall of their senior year in high school. Well, guess what! That's often not the case.

- Because a student must accept the early decision offer, she won't have an opportunity to compare that school's financial aid package with what other schools may have offered down the road. Of course, a school need not even offer as much aid to a student it knows will attend.

Because applying early decision or action can be risky, insist that other applications be almost ready to hit the mail in case that first-choice school says, "Thanks, but no thanks," or defers the decision until April.

No matter which form of admittance your youngster chooses, have him check the deadline dates for application submission. (Then, very quietly in the middle of the night, recheck those dates yourself.) Early admission deadlines are in the fall; the rest are in the winter, some at odd times like January 1. (Who's in the office then?) Some deadlines are measured by a postmark; others require the application be *in* the Admissions Office by a certain date. Make sure the deadlines you're noting are for the current year.

For many private colleges, applications are not a 25-minutes-and-back-to-my-computer-game task. They require teacher recommendations, sometimes a peer recommendation, and perhaps short and long essays. Makes you tired just thinking about it, doesn't it?

ON-TARGET RECOMMENDATIONS

Ask for recommendations from teachers who know your student, have given the student good grades, and are good writers. (Some very nice teachers write mush.)

Two days is not enough time to write a recommendation; two weeks is. But even with computers, some teachers refuse to write recommendations after a certain number of requests. Best advice: Ask early in the semester, whether or not your student has decided where she's applying.

Have your student give each teacher the recommendation form and a résumé. If your student is to pick up the recommendation, set a time to do that. If the teacher is to mail it to the college, provide a stamped, addressed envelope, and check back in two weeks to see if the teacher has mailed the recommendation.

Ask for recommendations from nonschool types like the guitar instructor, club soccer coach, church youth leader, or employer. (Does it go without saying that each of these people should actually like your kid?) Request that the writer note specifically how your youngster contributes to and how much time she spends on the activity.

(Ms. Manners reminder for your youngster: Hand-write a thank-you note to each person who took time to write a recommendation after applications are submitted.)

Unless your child has made a prize-winning video on an exceptional topic or is interested in a film or art major, skip the video. Most videos remind viewers of "How I Spent My Summer Vacation" and add clutter to the Admissions Office.

JUST GOTTA DO IT

Regardless of the type of application, certain chores must be handled. For example, remember when your youngster took the SAT and/or ACT those many months ago? Well, if she didn't request scores be sent to colleges where she's now applying, you'll pay an additional fee for each college that needs scores.

Haul out those accordion files full of test scores and application forms. They'll cut the time spent on completing applications in half because dates, numbers, and names will be handy.

Even when a college application says the essay is optional, encourage your student to write one anyway to show he can (that's something special these days!) and to set him apart from other applicants.

If your youngster is completing applications one at a time, prepare to hear a considerable amount of whining. That's because each application will be just a bit different from the next one, requiring your child to consistently engage in thinking, writing, and rewriting.

THE COMMON APPLICATION

That's not the case with the Common Application. A Common Application can be filled out once and sent to any of almost 200 institutions, mostly private, that accept it.

Some kids declare, "I'm not applying to any schools that won't accept the Common Application." Despite knowing it's a sorry process of elimination, you may have to shrug your shoulders, roll your eyes, and think, "That's one way to narrow choices."

Selective colleges probably will send an additional form requesting further information. And there are still those pesky financial aid applications to fill out for each school.

FINALLY—APPLICATION TIME

Before typing or writing on an application, make several copies. Then your youngster will have extras if by chance he makes mistakes. It's often easier to fill out one of the copies first to see how stuff fits in the boxes. Admissions directors appreciate neatness. One mistake won't send your student's application to the infamous round file, but it might push him back a few places in the race.

If typing the application isn't an option, have your child use a black or blue pen. (Just imagine that poor admissions director, faced with reading 15,000 forms!)

Be *acurit wit ur speling. Duh.*

Volunteer to proofread the application. Ask your child if there's anything in particular you should try to spot.

If it's a computer application, read a printout before transmitting the document or mailing a disk copy. Parents who grew up with pen in hand spot errors better on a paper than on a screen.

Caveats for computer apps: Sometimes, the computer genies running around in your hard drive get ornery and won't download the application. Or they make a meal of the completed or nearly completed application. You already know this, but backing up is key, here.

Suggest your student create two computer files, one for applications in progress and the other for applications completed and mailed. Your student can refer to materials in the latter file when filling out additional applications that seek similar information, as opposed to reinventing the wheel.

Always make a copy of each completed application and additional materials for your records.

Encourage your child—or volunteer—to create a master chart. For each college to which your child is applying, indicate on the chart the application deadline, who's writing recommendations and when they are picked up (or mailed), date the application is sent, and the response noting that the application arrived in the office.

SENDING THE APPLICATION

Whether or not your house is rife with procrastination, send the application packet either registered mail or certified mail, whatever is cheaper. Even then, we've heard war stories from parents who said they used certified mail, their packets never arrived, and they were not notified. Stick a self-addressed and stamped postcard inside the packet asking the college to notify you when the information arrives. Then, if you don't receive the postcard, call the Admissions Office.

"One short essay question asked if there was anything else our son wanted to tell the college. I suggested his sense of humor—which was fairly off-the-wall—didn't show in the application. So, instead of writing about it, he drew stick figures illustrating puns, and simply wrote that he liked puns. The college responded within a week that it was extremely interested in him."

Jim Adams

PROCRASTINATION AS AN ART FORM

"Procrastination comes from different reasons. Our youngster was very capable but feared rejection. She thought any college would reject her; any employer would reject her. We couldn't nag her. She'd work on her applications at 4:00 A.M., alone in her room. And you know what? She got them done!"

Dan Walker

"We finally set a rule: No cheerleading at Friday night's game if your essay draft isn't in our hands by Friday afternoon."

Janet Heimbuch

Sorting through the information, filling out the applications, and writing essays are processes your child needs to go through. It does no good for you to go through them instead—and it doesn't do much for your state of mind, either.

Get real. If your student can't prepare a college application, what is the kid going to do in college? (You're not going along as the roommate, are you?)

We adults have a tendency to want to get things done. If the student lags, we tend to take over.

Sometimes, the reason procrastination rears its ugly head is difficult to identify. Perhaps your student is afraid of being rejected or secretly dreads stepping away from the safe environs of high school.

Or maybe it's a horrible, stupid, ugly, who-cares-about-that-anyway essay question. Some selective colleges challenge students to write about unaccustomed topics: one favorite word, something they've outgrown that has influenced them, a TV sitcom pilot incorporating a soap opera, Enrico Fermi's personal trainer, van Gogh's ear. Some kids cheer and write such essays in two hours. Others agonize for two months and still aren't happy with the results.

Now's the time to think about why your student isn't moving forward, and the time to "listen" to what your student doesn't say, as much as what your student says. Helping your youngster see his way through here could win you the Patient Parent of the Year Award. Consider:

1. Ease the pressure by lightening up on household chores. Kids already are busy just because it's senior year.
2. Post deadlines on the refrigerator door.
3. Share your own schedule with your youngster, indicating when you can and can't help.

The ultimate fix for procrastinators: Overnight delivery service is about $15; even then, some don't guarantee overnight delivery.

VOICES OF EXPERIENCE

"Our son put off and put off and put off. Finally, we told him, 'The Army, the Navy, and the Marines are all calling you. You are going somewhere in the fall after you graduate. It can be school or it can be the Army, Navy, or the Marines. But you are going somewhere.' "

Susie Polden

"A guidance counselor said we shouldn't nag our youngster to get the application in. The counselor believed if a student couldn't meet the deadline, he or she probably isn't mature enough to be going to college right now."

Lee Galles

WHOSE ESSAY IS IT ANYWAY?

Okay, your youngster has put it off, ignored your hints to get busy, and carried procrastination to new heights. We're talking about writing the essay. And usually, it's not just one essay that needs writing; it's more like a big one and two, three, or maybe four little ones. What's a parent to do? Look at the following list of 16 rules for writing the essay. Talk generally about the essay with your youngster, covering topics and writing points. Then, while your student is actually working on the project, go fix leaky faucets.

- **RULE NO. 1. REMEMBER THE READER.** Admissions people probably read what seems like a million essays. That's tough, even if you are getting paid! Your child's essay should be interesting, neat, grammatically correct, and to the point.

- **RULE NO. 2. HOOK THE READER WITH THE FIRST SENTENCE.** It should be 30 words or less and should sum up the writer's feeling, philosophy, or point of the whole essay. Sometimes, the hook sentence gets buried deeper in the essay. If you think the beginning seems slow, look to the second paragraph, where the meat of the article is usually located. If you find a sharp, grab-'em-by-the-throat-and-make-'em-read beginning there, suggest it become the first sentence.

- **RULE NO. 3. SELLING THYSELF.** The reader already knows your student's test scores, activities, and birth date from the fill-in-the-blank parts of the application. The essay must say something personal that doesn't require repeating the basics. But not too personal. This isn't writing therapy.

- **RULE NO. 4. WHOSE ESSAY IS THIS ANYWAY?** This may be hard to remember, but it isn't your essay. Still, you may offer suggestions. Recall some of the wonderful things the child has done; list special characteristics; talk about what makes your youngster different from everybody else. In the end, however, what the child chooses to write about becomes his or her decision.

- **RULE NO. 5. MORE OF WHOSE-ESSAY-IS-THIS-ANYWAY?** There are web sites for essay critiquing, for a fee, of course. But your student's English teacher or counselor probably can be as good a resource. They know your child and how your child writes. College admission officers can pretty well spot highly doctored essays.

- **RULE NO. 6. WRITE ABOUT SOMETHING NO ONE ELSE WILL WRITE ABOUT.** Sports are okay, football isn't—too common. But has your youngster done a triathlon? Gone kayaking? Speed-skating? Rock climbing? And has the sportster won state, regional, or national awards?

- **RULE NO. 7. THINK COMMUNITY SERVICE.** The college folks want to educate your student, but they also want to know what your student can do for the college. They like reading about humanitarian work because down the road they're hoping your student will work for them as well.

- **RULE NO. 8. THINK PASSION (TO A POINT).** It isn't just about community service anymore. College folks smile fondly upon students who pursue a particular activity with a passion. Doing that requires focus, perseverance, and singularity of purpose, all qualities reflective of students the college is courting. Examples: Starting your own lawn-mowing business, getting peers to go to city council meetings to request a skateboarding section in the park, working on political campaigns, writing songs, entering artwork in shows—you get the idea.

- **RULE NO. 9. SKIP THE TRAVELOGUE.** The reader isn't buying a trip. Eye-catching essays focus on an incident or person on the trip who made such an indelible impression on your child that your youngster now fasts one day a week and helps in the local food pantry.

- **RULE NO. 10. SKIP THE IRRELEVANT.** Just because your student remembers everything about an event doesn't mean she has to tell all. It's like picking out red jellybeans from the bowl because they are the brightest and taste the best. Say whatchagotta say and stop.

- **RULE NO. 11. STOP TRYING TO FIGURE OUT WHAT "THEY" WANT.** There's no one right answer to any essay question. "They" want to know what interests your child, why, and how it makes your youngster feel and think.

- **RULE NO. 12. COUNTER STEREOTYPES.** There's nothing like turning a stereotype inside out to get a college's attention. So if your daughter—not your son—is the football team's placekicker, she's gotta write about it. And if your son—not your daughter—pays weekly visits to a nursing home, it's worth mentioning.

- **RULE NO. 13. GOOD WRITERS WRITE THE WAY THEY SPEAK.** The college won't be impressed with gargantuan words not ordinarily used. They only make the essay sound pretentious and phony.

- **RULE NO. 14. REWRITE, REWRITE, REWRITE.** Tell your writer this little surprise before he starts writing: The first thing he writes won't be the final product. After all, playing a new piece of music, mastering a new soccer technique, or doing a first read-through of the school play aren't nearly as good as the final performance. Figure on three rewrites.

- **RULE NO. 15. READING TO ONESELF.** If your youngster reads her own essay out loud to herself, she'll hear weird sentences, missing words, and poor grammar. (It works for adults as well as kids.)

- **RULE NO. 16. IF YOU'RE ASKED TO READ THE ESSAY.** Be considerate and nonjudgmental. Let your student make the writing decisions. You ask questions that identify weak areas: Can you put this another way? Exactly what do you mean here? Is this the best word to use? Could this sentence be shorter? Could you tell a bit more about this thought? What's the main thought you want your reader to remember?

CHAPTER 8

LEARNING DISABILITIES— MAPPING COLLEGE DREAMS

L earning disabilities (LD) don't disappear at the college gate. That's why it's so important to get students with learning disabilities into the right college. The process may take a few different turns in the road. Here's a map to figure out the if, how, and where, beginning with those all-important high school days.

WHAT ARE LEARNING DISABILITIES ANYWAY?

VOICES OF EXPERIENCE

"I didn't know until mid-December of our daughter's senior year that she was dyslexic—and I'm even a teacher! She had taken the ACT four times and her score was 17. We spent a total $2,300 for help between the first and last ACT test and nothing changed."

Barb Zurek

"Parents and teachers get fooled with learning disabilities. It's like a wire that trips: Some days it's in and some days it's out; they can do some subjects and not others."

M. Kathleen Heikkila, Associate Professor of Education, Graceland College, Lamoni, Iowa

Learning disabilities are permanent disorders that affect the way students with normal or above-average intelligence take in, interpret, retain, and express information. Like interference on the radio or a fuzzy TV picture, incoming or outgoing information may become scrambled as it travels between the eye, ear, or skin and the brain.

By law, students diagnosed with LD must have IQs that fall in the average to above-average range and show a discrepancy between potential and performance on achievement tests. Even though the student may be below average in schoolwork, he may exhibit strengths in one area and weaknesses in another.

For kids with learning disabilities, it isn't a not-so-smart problem; it's a processing problem.

Commonly recognized learning disabilities center around reading comprehension, verbal-auditory comprehension, spelling, written expression, math computation, and problem solving. Less frequent learning disabilities include having trouble with organizational skills, time management, and social skills.

Attention Deficit Disorder is not a learning disability because it does not affect how students process information, but it is a disability that has accommodations requirements.

LD is the most predominant disability of all special needs on today's college campus. The main learning disability is *dyslexia*, which is mixing up letter order. There's also *dyscalculia* (the student can't do math), processing reading and/or math, and short- and long-term memory deficits.

Learning disabilities aren't consistent. Your child may do just fine on Monday and not so fine on Tuesday. Your child may have experienced difficulties in grade school, do okay in high school, then go back to struggling in college. Disabilities seem to appear and disappear, but they usually never go away. (You're right, it's not fair.)

You can recall times when your child did well academically. So you say, "Hey, you can do this if you just put your mind to it. You've done it before!" Such encouragement is well intentioned but won't get the job done. If a particular learning switch is turned off because your child's method of learning isn't understood or addressed, or because she doesn't understand the information or how to proceed, study, memorize, or use resources, she can "just put her mind to it" all she wants and she still will not succeed.

It's imperative that you and your child understand your youngster's learning disability—his individual strengths and weaknesses. That helps you provide the right support. And it helps your child realize that he isn't stupid.

The self-esteem aspect is critical for kids with LD because they experience so much stress, frustration, and failure and usually can't recognize their own gifts. Building self-esteem is accomplished partly through making sure educational needs are identified and met. But no matter how hard you work, remember you can't ensure that someone, be it a teacher or another student, won't refer to your child as "stupid."

VOICES OF EXPERIENCE

"We had a roller coaster child. He was diagnosed with a learning disability and was in a self-contained class based on his Individual Education Plan. He did well and was mainstreamed. Special programs were provided and again he did well. As a result, he lost the support services and ended up falling downward and struggling in class."

Cathy Belter

STILL BEING THE ADVOCATE—SORT OF

VOICES OF EXPERIENCE

"Moms generally take the lead role (in dealing with LD educational issues). I took the school role and (his father) took the Boy Scout leader role. When our son went before a panel for his Eagle Scout rank, he talked about being an LD student. The panel never had a child identify himself like that before. They were so impressed they kept him for a long time, asking questions. Meanwhile, his dad was pacing back and forth outside, thinking his son had not made Eagle Scout."

Susie Edwards

"I believe you should go through administrative review if an issue is in dispute. My personality is to go into the process with honey. If you are screeching in someone's face, no one will listen to you. They will start to protect themselves, which is natural. Start talking first about what is going right, then what is not going right. Criticism wrapped in praise gets you further."

Pam Broome, Educational Consultant, Springfield, Virginia

Just because your youngster is in the nearly adult world of high school doesn't mean you'll finally be able to get off that guilt trip you've been on ever since the child's disabilities were diagnosed. It doesn't do a bit of good, but parents of children with LD seem to forever ask themselves, "Why didn't I test my child earlier? Why didn't I push for help sooner?"

It's not unusual for parents to feel disenchanted with the education system. Certainly, not all teachers and administrators are equally receptive, knowledgeable, and/or adept at identifying students with learning disabilities. Indeed, many students are not properly identified until high school and even college. Parents must not be discouraged from pursuing answers to their questions about their child's academic performance. In fact, they must be proactive.

So you keep advocating, but with a new emphasis. Realize that the responsibility for advocacy now must begin shifting from you to your child. Parents who don't recognize the importance of that shift risk creating an adult-child so dependent upon them that the youngster never does realize the benefits of advocating for himself.

INDIVIDUALIZED EDUCATION PROGRAM (IEP) POWER

Knowledge is power. And kids who know about and understand their IEPs are more powerful.

Each IEP lists the accommodations your student needs. It includes, but isn't limited to a scribe, reader, or tutor; a copy of class notes prior to class; extended time for tests and in-class assignments; a tape recorder or book with enlarged text.

By now, your child must be able to recognize and understand her strengths and weaknesses, which will happen when she knows her IEP. A student should be able to say to the teacher, "Here's what I do well in your class. Here's what I don't understand. Could you teach it to me in a different way?"

The IEP always should be seen as a tool, not a crutch. It should be handled with diplomacy. For example, your student needs to realize that teachers and other students will not react well to hearing an "I-have-to-have-special-privileges-in-this-class" mantra, even though they are prescribed in the IEP. Quietly making sure that the right things are happening is preferable.

You and your child should attend every IEP conference together, and your child should be the one asking and answering questions. Students who lead their own conferences learn to understand and come to grips with their learning disability rather than be ashamed of it.

Ideally, participants share ideas, with the emphasis always and only on helping the student. And the conference language is plain English rather than "educationese" that only the educators fully comprehend.

Between conferences, if there appears to be a problem with how your child or a teacher is interpreting the IEP, request a three-way conference for you, the child, and the teacher.

But even as you shift advocacy responsibility to your child, your involvement is crucial in the transition from high school to college. That is too important for your child to handle alone. In fact, parent and child together can't get the job done. It takes a whole team.

Most likely, the active parent advocate with school LD issues is and will remain mom. We hear that many, but certainly not all, dads have a tough time accepting the learning disability thing in the first place and, consequently, do other activities with the child where the LD isn't such a factor.

Some parents seek support in a local parent advocacy group; others feel uncomfortable reaching out and sharing. After all, the agenda for a group of parents with children with LD is very different from the agenda for a group of band parents. With the latter, everybody's working together to send the kids off to the Rose Bowl Parade. With the former, every child, and every parent, has a pressing, individual goal first.

Bottom line basics for parents, even when everything appears rosy with the child's progress:

A. Learn the laws and rules governing special needs education (see Getting Down to Basics—Your Rights, the Law at the end of this chapter).
B. Keep a notebook or journal for dated notes of conversations and documentation of every phone call, every meeting.
C. Write down your child's actions to demonstrate his pattern of speech or behavior.
D. Keep copies of IEPs, testing results, work samples, and teacher reports.
E. Make any request for information or action in writing. You must leave a paper trail.

Whew, advocating for your student with learning disabilities, and teaching your student to self-advocate, is almost like a full-time job when you consider what you have to learn about the disability, the law, and how your child's educational and emotional needs are met.

Although parents usually don't yell, "Sue them!" at the first sign of differences with the school, some find litigation is the answer when they have exhausted the administrative process. It's an individual decision for a specific situation.

VOICES OF EXPERIENCE

"When the child is present at the IEP conference, he becomes accustomed to talking with people who care about him and about how he can be successful in school. Together, they set goals and objectives for the year and discuss techniques and accommodations that will help him in his classes. Also, the IEP conference can be a reality check for parents. While they may go in hoping the school can fix their child's difficulties, the reality is that the disability is not going to go away. This is a fact that parents must learn to accept and often that is not easy."

Liz DeMik

"When I appealed for my child to be labeled LD, the phraseology I used led the school to put her in one of ten categories available. I didn't even know there were ten categories. During discussions, it became apparent to administrators that she should have been in a different category, but officials simply said she didn't qualify. When I appealed to the Board of Education, they told the high school to change her category and reconsider, which is when she received her classification. I didn't learn of the ten categories until the appeal response came back to me. It is to the cost-benefit of the school not to help. One more point: The Board of Education said my appeal letter was one of the best they had seen. I share that not to brag, but to point out that it takes an educated person to get through the system."

Claudia Harkins

IS YOUR CHILD ABLE TO GO TO COLLEGE?

VOICES OF EXPERIENCE

"When I counsel a young person who is having difficulties academically, the student will say, 'Well, I thought maybe in college I wouldn't need the accommodations. I thought maybe this time I could take the multiple-choice test, like everybody else. I just want to be normal.' "

Marcy McGahee-Kovac, Special Education Teacher, Fairfax County Public Schools, Virginia

"On campus tours it's important for students and parents to talk separately with whoever is in charge of services for special needs students. At our college, I often visit with students who don't know their specific disability or the types of services they'll need. It's clear Mom and the educators had talked and the student wasn't involved in the process. How will the students suddenly cope without that knowledge?"

M. Kathleen Heikkila

Is your child able to go to college? That's a huge question—one that must be dealt with long before the cap and gown are ordered.

Answering the question isn't easy. No matter how bright your child, learning disabilities will affect her ability to perform. Also, the disabilities already may have convinced her that she's stupid. She's not, but that may be her perception, and there's that thing about perception and reality.

You may want your child to go to college, but does the child want to? A majority of students with LD don't return for their sophomore year. Some reasons:

—The student didn't accept the fact that a disability existed.
—The student didn't know what accommodations were available and/or what he needed.
—The student didn't request accommodations.

—The student didn't recognize how she learns best.
—The student didn't learn or apply effective study and time-management strategies.

Aside from testing, there are things you can do to begin building a base of information that will help determine if your youngster can succeed in college. Try to:

- Volunteer in your high school guidance counseling office so you can learn more about college in general and specific colleges that do well by students with LD.
- Get friendly with the counselors.
- Listen to what educators involved with students with LD have to say.
- Communicate with a variety of college students who have disabilities and are experiencing success; if the students aren't around, talk with their parents.
- Contact the National Information Center for Children and Youth with Disabilities at *www.nichcy.org*
- Log on to LDOnLine, an interactive guide to learning disabilities, at *www.ldonline.com*
- Join a parent support group or talk parent-to-parent.

If you and/or your youngster have college aspirations, begin the quest for the right college the day he's a freshman in high school. He needs to understand that high school is serious business from the get-go for all kids, but even more so for kids with learning disabilities. You both should become familiar as quickly as possible with required courses for high school graduation, admission requirements for state colleges, and the standardized testing process for college applications.

High school students memorize fact after fact after fact, take test after test after test, and go to one class after another, day after day after day. In college, classes do not meet every day and tests are not as frequent. But there is much more information to process and standards for applying the information are higher. Realizing those differences can be a big step toward helping your youngster consider that college may be possible if the course load is carefully planned.

Maybe your youngster could take a college course for high school and college credit while she's in high school. Experiencing that different pace firsthand might get a student with LD enthusiastic about attending college after high school.

Think about options, such as going the first year to a hometown or nearby college where your student can live on campus but still work with his high school tutors, assuming they're qualified for college tutoring.

Or, take only a couple of courses the first few semesters of college. This does present a couple of red flags:

a) If you expect financial aid, ask colleges how many courses a student must take in a semester to qualify for aid. Usually, aid eligibility differs for full- and part-time students;

b) It's expensive to take light loads at a private college because it then will require more than four years to graduate.

If your child elects to take a "full load," make sure it is balanced, including courses that reflect your child's interests. There is nothing worse for a youngster with reading disabilities than to take 15 hours of courses that require hours of reading. Instead, add in a math, music, or PE course, or something related to your child's major.

"Whether your child goes to college or not, you will continue to be on an emotional trip. It is forever. It is your life. It is not fair, but the fact is that society will not make exceptions for your child."

Susie Edwards

"Sometimes it is difficult for parents to be realistic about their child's ability to go to college because they have dreams for their child's future and they instill them in their son or daughter at an early age."

Marcy McGahee-Kovac

THE FIRST TEAM—THE TEACHERS, YOUR CHILD, AND YOU

"We got a syllabus from every high school teacher. Then our daughter and I would write what's due when on the calendar together. Plus, each of her teachers sent comments home to me every Friday. I realized that when our daughter would go to college, she'd be on her own, but at least we gave her an operating pattern."

Barb Zurek

"Our daughter was tested in high school. When they identified her learning disability, I said, 'Now, aren't you glad there is something we can work on?' She replied, 'No, I just want to be normal.' I had to tell her that it was never going to be normal for her. That life would always be this way."

Claudia Harkins

Even though high school dances are fun and organizing homework isn't, the road to college has to be paved with more than good intentions for getting schoolwork done acceptably. That's where the parent, teachers, and student can work together.

You can be your child's teacher/tutor or your child's parent, but you most likely can't be both. And you can't really delegate that parent role even if you'd like to, so it's probably best if you settle in and work with the teacher/tutor.

If your student has difficulty handling high school work, don't get angry with the teacher for not "fixing" the problem. Blaming the teacher didn't make the problem go away in elementary or middle school, and it won't work in high school, either.

Take the positive road. Stay in close contact with each teacher via e-mail.

Occasionally, send a little thank-you note to the teachers for helping your child. Elementary teachers get thank-you notes all the time; that's not true with secondary teachers.

Ask the counselor to pull all of your child's teachers together for a conference each semester. The math teacher's take on your youngster may go one direction and the English teacher's take, another. Each teacher is seeing a totally different view of your child. The conference will help them to see the whole child, and perhaps the experience will provide insights to teaching methods others are using that work better for your child.

THE COMPUTER

The computer—that supposed answer to almost all learning problems—actually may make learning more difficult for a child with a learning disability—especially if it's hard for the student to read the screen and he has problems following the order of command cues or learns best by listening. Talk with teachers who rely heavily on computers in the classroom to make sure your youngster is responding favorably.

Experiment with background color and font size on the computer to see what works best for your child. Also, watch for new software that helps students to compensate for disabilities. Share information about software with teachers, and they'll share with you.

Teachers need to understand that having accommodations does not give the student an unfair advantage. Rather, accommodations bring the child to the level at which other students already operate.

You expect to find support from the special education or resource room teacher, but regular classroom teachers are equally responsible for assisting children. They, too, will become part of a support system.

If you decide to hire a tutor for schoolwork or standardized tests, ask for recommendations from the special ed teachers or other parents. But, of course, you'll still check credentials, experience, references, results, and how many students with your child's type of special need the tutor has assisted.

"I chose teachers based on my child's learning styles. My children needed to be with caring teachers who provided real-world, hands-on, visual learning experiences."

Pamela Broome

"At our school's Meet the Teacher Night, the art teacher in period seven told parents to let her know if their child needed to sit close to the front of the room for any reason. Not one teacher in the first six periods had ever mentioned that."

Nancy Jones

BECOMING BEST FRIENDS WITH THE COUNSELOR

"Our daughter took a planning test in high school to see what she could do when she grew up. On the test, she asked for specific help with language arts, comprehension, and reading. The school never picked up on that or reported it to us. We know now that even if your kid is in high school, she's still a kid and needs your guidance."

Barb Zurek

Request a counselor you trust, someone who wants to see your child succeed but won't be involved at the emotional level upon which you're operating. Connecting with this person may take some assertiveness on your part, but it's worth the effort. The counselor can help craft the difference between success and failure in your child's high school career and college expectations.

High school is a different animal. It's probably the biggest school your child has attended—and the most impersonal. (Big and impersonal often go together.) Depending upon how big BIG is, the principal may never know your student or you. That's why the counselor's guidance and support are crucial.

Counselors offer suggestions. So do parents. The difference is that high school students are more likely to listen to suggestions when they come from the counselor, or from just about any adult in the world besides you. Ah, but you may have noticed that already.

If your student won't discuss goals and expectations beyond high school with you (most likely because you're the parent and don't know anything), encourage your youngster to talk with the counselor. Or ask the counselor to seek him out.

A transition plan for the student's goals either for further education or employment is required to be part of the IEP once the student reaches age 14. But planning for college needs to start earlier.

Ideally, such discussions happen in eighth grade so your child is properly placed in classes the moment she steps into ninth grade. But we all know "ideally" often is beyond our control. Get to it ASAP, then. You know education stuff just takes longer to happen with your student.

A good counselor will encourage your child to get involved in an activity or two. That can do so much for students with learning disabilities who often don't feel good about themselves and won't join unless urged to.

Selecting the right teachers for your student is paramount, and counselors know their teachers. It's sad but true that some teachers still say, "This is how we do things in my classroom. Period." Such an approach does not cause students with LD to flourish.

As long as you're inquiring about good teachers, ask older students what they think. They know who's good and who isn't, and they'll tell you!

Even very good counselors don't know everything. The vast majority have only a smattering of knowledge about special education needs. Since your child's transition plan from high school to college is so important, you'll want to work with the counselor and a special ed teacher.

If you have a sense something may be wrong, even though the school has tested your child, hunt for a private education counselor specializing in learning disabilities. Yes, that costs money and not everyone can afford it. There's no good answer to that unfairness in life.

If you opt for an outside testing agency or consultant, shop around. There's a huge variety in cost as well as credentials of those doing the testing. Ask parents of other students with LD for recommendations.

TESTING. TESTING.

"I tell the LD students I tutor that if their parents are paying me to prepare them simply to take a test, it will be a waste of their money. The students need to learn how to think, to organize, and to 'learn how to learn,' whatever the occasion. Developing those skills gives students a sense that learning is worth their time. Parents need to seek out teachers and tutors who care more about skill development than about test scores."

Cindy Finch, Special Education Teacher, Shaker Heights, Ohio

One of your high school goals must be to ensure appropriate testing and documentation of your student's needs before she takes standardized tests and applies for college.

STANDARDIZED TESTS

Too often, instead of a student with LD taking SAT and/or ACT college entrance tests, the tests take the student. The best source of information about what specific kind of help a student needs is the special ed teacher along with the student's previous experience with standardized test taking.

Your school should provide comprehensive testing to diagnose a learning disability. Some parents request the testing during freshman year because it may point out accommodations necessary for classroom use and with the ACT/SAT. Others want it in twelfth grade so that it's as current as possible. (A student may be retested at any time.) The testing must be conducted within three years of attending college for the student to receive accommodations in college.

Still, your rule should be: Assume nothing. Check with each college for its requirements to document a learning disability to make sure you are all playing by the same rules. These can differ in higher education from secondary education.

Any test-taking accommodations must be updated in the IEP. Verbal commitments or discussions about accommodations just won't do it for the required documentation for standardized testing.

A student can't request accommodations on standardized tests for college entrance unless the student is using the accommodations in the classroom. Having an IEP, 504 Plan, or professional evaluation does *not* guarantee eligibility for SAT/ACT testing accommodations. Check early for precise requirements for test registration and work with your counselor to ensure compliance.

Encourage your child to take all the practice and college entrance tests: the PSAT, PLAN, SAT, and ACT. That allows her to practice and hone skills. Also, understanding a test's format gets the student beyond that feeling of panic about the unknown (see Chapter 5).

Always take the tests with accommodations as prescribed in the IEP. You may need to remind your student that the accommodations are not giving him a better chance to score well on the exam; instead, they're giving him an equal chance.

TEST PREP CLASSES

Many students with and without disabilities seek to improve test scores by taking test prep classes. Some parents of students with disabilities opt for an individual tutor who understands which teaching methods work best for a particular disability. Either way, it's expensive, but probably worth it for confidence and learning test-taking strategies and skills.

Bring the tutor a copy of your student's PSAT score, comprehensive testing report, and IEP. (That's a lot of alphabet stuff, isn't it!) The PSAT score will help pinpoint weak areas to work on for the SAT. The testing report and IEP will show which accommodations the student needs. Then make sure the tutor abides by the accommodations.

If your student responds out loud to questions in a practice session, the tutor can hear his method of thinking and evaluate how he maneuvers through the answering process.

TEST-TAKING TIPS TO TALK ABOUT WITH YOUR STUDENT

A. Don't take the same practice tests over and over again. Memorization will replace skill development.
B. Practice taking both the SAT and the ACT. If the colleges to which your child is applying require one test as opposed to the other, place the emphasis there.

C. If you enroll your youngster in a test preparation review class or hire a tutor, try to time finishing the class a week before taking the SAT or ACT for the second time.
D. Some Internet sites have a practice test. Also, you can buy software with practice tests for home computer use, and the guidance office may have software for practice tests to use at school.
E. Choose a test site that's either in the student's school or as close as possible. It's less stressful to take the tests in familiar surroundings, and traveling then doesn't become another part of the event.

The only opportunity any student has to be considered for a National Merit Scholarship is to take the PSAT in the junior year. Even if your student doesn't get one—and most students don't—it's another practice opportunity and colleges will begin sending lots of brochures.

When to take the SAT and ACT takes planning because not all accommodations are allowed on all test dates and sites. Additionally, students need to finish as much math coursework as possible before taking the SAT and/or ACT for real rather than just practice. Test dates are available on web sites (*www.collegeboard.org* and *www.act.org*) or in the high school counseling office.

Students with learning disabilities must register for the SAT and/or ACT by regular mail because they must include documentation for requested accommodations. That's definitely not a wait-till-the-last-minute chore.

SUGGESTED TIMETABLE REGARDING STANDARDIZED AND ACCOMMODATIONS TESTING

- Ninth grade:
  1. Check that test-taking accommodations are updated in the IEP.
- Tenth grade:
  1. Retake comprehensive testing if needed to update accommodations for standardized tests.
  2. Take the PSAT and PLAN. Scores don't count for college admission but do indicate strong and weak areas.
- Eleventh grade:
  1. Check again; are accommodations updated and documented in the IEP?
  2. Take the PSAT in the fall for practice and to qualify for the National Merit Scholarship Corporation program.
  3. Check early in August or September for dates to take the SAT and ACT during junior year. Not all types of accommodations are allowed on all test dates.

4. Take the SAT and ACT in the spring, when students have finished most of the eleventh grade algebra covered on the tests.

- Twelfth grade:

    1. Register early and retake the SAT and ACT early in the fall and/or before the winter holidays to meet the application deadlines of most colleges. Of course, check the application deadlines of your child's particular college choices.

    2. Request a final comprehensive testing, if necessary.

"Don't test the child to find out whether she is bright or dumb. Test the child to find out her dreams."

Marcy McGahee-Kovac

FERRETING OUT USER-FRIENDLY COLLEGES

"If you compare the college that charges for resource support with one that has resource support built into its program, philosophically the two schools are worlds apart."

Diane Lenahan

"Don't visit a school you know your child can't succeed in as a student. Your youngster may fall in love with the place and then be disappointed."

Claudia Harkins

"We were naive. We thought that when a college said it had support services, everything was okay. But when our son enrolled, the services were done by upper-level students who were constantly changing. Our son needed consistency. It was okay the first year. Then everything collapsed for him after the holidays his second year. He dropped out of college for six months; then, after three days of testing, he showed a broad range of college abilities. But he needed to have real services at college."

Cathy Belter

The amount of literature colleges send to high school students is enough to bury a small person. For a student with learning disabilities, the pile can be overwhelming.

Suggest your student divide the literature into two piles—one for colleges that offer identified services and a second for colleges that do not. Then suggest that everything in the second pile be thrown away.

Colleges provide LD services that range from the VW to the Cadillac. Here are lots of questions to ask to evaluate the strength of each college's LD support program:

- Does the college material and its web site list specific LD services? How about a campus chat room for students with LD?

- Who is in charge of the LD program and what are that person's credentials? Is the program stronger than just one person? Having a charismatic director with a limp-noodle staff isn't good, especially if the director leaves when your child is halfway through college.

- How specifically does the LD director or counselor work with students? Does he advise about class selection, knowing which professors deal well with accommodations? Does he advocate for your student with professors who don't understand your student's needs despite the student explaining the needs?

- Who evaluates the applications of students with learning disabilities? If it's the Admissions Office, there should be evaluation assistance from support services.

- Is an LD study skills class part of the curriculum?

- Will your child be expected to attend homework study halls?

- Will your child be required to spend time in the LD department on a regular basis?

- How does the LD staff work with departmental advisors?

- Will your student's advisor assist your youngster in selecting professors, based upon her learning style?

- What about alternative testing procedures?

- What about tutorial services in reading, math, oral expression, listening comprehension, social studies, history, foreign language, and science?

- What are the hours of service?

- Is counseling and testing available on campus if the student has difficulties? What are the credentials of those campus professionals?

- What's the teacher-student tutoring ratio? Are tutors certified and knowledgeable about how to work with your student's learning disability? Will your student go to the same tutor or will tutors be assigned from a pool as available?

- Is there a "bridge" program that gives students with LD a jump-start by beginning school a bit ahead of everybody else? Usually, such programs center around reviewing the basic skills of reading, writing, and math.

- What are the curriculum requirements in your child's area of study? Are there tons of prerequisites or can your student get into core courses right away? What are the requirements to qualify for an exemption from a required course in the curriculum?

- Does the school's course booklet include descriptions of teaching styles?

- Do students with LD get first pick of classes? (FYI: Sometimes athletes do!)

- Is there a student support group on campus?

- Is there a parent support group?

- How do campus living arrangements relate to your child's disability? For example, can he work on a voice-directed computer in the dorm room, at midnight?

One more thing: Sometimes, professors engaged in research won't allow students to tape their lectures because of copyright issues. Sounds innocuous but it isn't for a student who needs information taped.

> "Our high school principal knew us so well that she would ask, 'What classes does your son want to take? Let me see who should teach them.' That's the same thing that the LD counselor at college should do for your child."
>
> **Pamela Broome**

TWISTS AND TURNS IN THE LD APPLICATION PROCESS

> "In his cover letters, our son said he was an 'identified LD student.' Then, he pointed out his strengths and weaknesses. For example, he discussed his D+ in Spanish because he knew the Admissions Office would notice it anyway."
>
> **Susie Edwards**

It's nice to meet the college president while you're visiting the campus, but meeting the director of the LD program is imperative. And if the director shares that she was once told she would never succeed because she had a learning disability, lucky your student!

Basically, if you don't make an appointment with the director before you show up on campus, you have no business showing up on campus.

The campus interview is critical. It allows your student to demonstrate what he knows about his diagnosis, testing, IEP, and services he needs. Just be sure he brings all those records with him.

Encourage your student to discuss his strengths that don't show in his GPA during the interview. For example, "My English grades are low because I score poorly on essay tests. But my math grades show I can achieve and that's the area I want to study here." If colleges know about a student's learning disability, they can deviate from their standard admissions formula and apply alternative criteria that take into account your student's strengths.

During the interview, don't request unneeded accommodations. For example, if your child has never used a scribe before, don't ask for a scribe. The same goes for the application and with professors during the year.

College web sites may indicate there are services for students with learning disabilities or other special needs. But students and parents still must personally contact each school to ask pertinent questions to evaluate services.

With rolling admission, your student will learn early in senior year if he has been admitted to a particular college. Emotionally, that becomes a huge ego booster when all the other kids are talking about going to college and your child can chime right in. Even if he ends up attending another college, the application will have been worth the effort.

No matter how perfect the college may seem, in most cases, until your student steps forward and says, "I need help," nothing will happen.

VOICES OF EXPERIENCE

"My requirement was that my child not apply to any college that required her to write an essay because, in the end, I'm the one who would write it."

Claudia Harkins

"My husband and our son met with the chair of the learning disabilities program during one of their campus visits. The department chair kept asking my husband questions about our son's learning disabilities, and our son kept answering the questions. Finally, the man stopped and said, 'I have never had a student come in and talk about his strengths and weaknesses and needs like this before.' "

Susie Edwards

BEFORE AND BEYOND GRADUATION

Your student will come down with a severe case of senioritis, just like all the other kids. The problem, however, is that all the other kids may be doing better academically. They can party hard, procrastinate, space out, and still pull their grades out. For some kids with learning disabilities, that's a quantum leap. You may want to hire a tutor to combat senioritis.

Carefully check your child's accommodations list before you sign off and the high school forwards the information to colleges. Sometimes, accommodations aren't accurate, or your youngster has outgrown a particular prescription. Be aware of different accommodations that might be needed for some college classes.

You have always been looking over the teacher's shoulder. In college, you cannot look over the professor's shoulder because, quite simply, you aren't there. That may be a major adjustment, for you as well as your student.

Some children with learning disabilities struggle with organization, and almost all have a real sense of nesting. Don't just walk into the dorm room, plop down suitcases and boxes, and say, "Hey, let's go eat!" Be clear with the college official in charge of people moving that you need ample time to help your child move in and get settled. (Those are two different things.)

A new place, new people, new professors—lots of anxiety-inducing stuff to begin college. Your student may wonder: "What's going to happen when Mom and Dad leave?" Tell your student, whether or not she asks: "Leave your door open and people will come in and visit. Do activities to get integrated. We love you."

There's no guarantee that a youngster will go off to college, study hard for four years and graduate, no matter who the kid or which college. But students with LD have more need for breathers along the way. If your youngster calls home announcing that she'd like to experience the real world for a while before finishing college, don't panic. Think about it as an opportunity for some meaningful work experience as your youngster works, pays rent, and all that good stuff.

Finally, encouraging your child to identify his talents and interests goes a long way toward seeing the youngster graduate from college feeling prepared and confident to go to work.

VOICES OF EXPERIENCE

"My daughter has learned she must study longer hours than anyone else. She has great determination, works really hard, and talks to her professors. She will graduate in June with a psychology major and has had two internships. I'm very proud of her—she would just keep fighting. She's not stupid. She just learns in a different way."

Jerry Rewa

GETTING DOWN TO BASICS—YOUR RIGHTS, THE LAW

Federal legislation requires any school, college, or university receiving federal financial assistance (which is almost all of them) to make accommodations for students with learning disabilities. They may include adaptations in the way specific courses are conducted, the use of auxiliary equipment and support staff, and modifications in academic requirements. Such aids or services should be selected in consultation with the student who will use them.

LEGISLATION

Basically, there are three pieces of legislation that specifically address your child's right to an education:

- **SECTION 504 OF THE REHABILITATION ACT OF 1973.** As amended through 1992, Section 504 states that an institution must not discriminate in the recruitment, admission, or treatment of students. Students with documented disabilities may request modifications, accommodations, or auxiliary aids that will enable them to participate in and benefit from all postsecondary educational programs and activities. Postsecondary institutions must make such changes to ensure that the academic program is accessible to the greatest extent possible by all students with disabilities. The legislation includes a long list of prohibitions, such as limiting the number of students with disabilities that it will admit, excluding a qualified student with a disability from any course of study, and using admissions tests or criteria that inadequately measure the academic qualifications of disabled students because special provisions weren't made for the student.

- **THE AMERICANS WITH DISABILITIES ACT OF 1990.** This act upholds and extends the standards for compliance set forth in Section 504 to employment practices, communications, and all policies, procedures, and practices that impact on the treatment of students with disabilities.

- **THE INDIVIDUALIZED EDUCATION PROGRAM (IEP) OF THE INDIVIDUALS WITH DISABILITIES EDUCATION ACT.** This guarantees services to students with documented disabilities in kindergarten through twelfth grade. Those services are outlined in the student's IEP, which is updated annually until the student receives a high school diploma. Additionally, services to help the student make a transition from high school to a college or university must begin no later than age 14, and must be included in the IEP.

Those three laws insure that, from kindergarten through twelfth grade, students with documented disabilities receive appropriate services as outlined in the IEP. The IEP is put together and updated annually or as needed by a team that includes educators, parents and student, and others as appropriate. Also, documentation of the disability that is provided to postsecondary institutions must be no more than three years old. At the postsecondary level, the level of assistance that students with documented disabilities receive should be negotiated with the institution and can become a very complex issue. Best advice for parents of students going into or already in college: Leave paper trails everywhere.

CHAPTER 9
SENIORITIS—IS IT CURABLE?

Sign, seal, and mail those applications and guess what happens? Nothing and everything, as your senior's motivation and willpower evaporate. Here are tips on how to deal with seniors, the wait for acceptance or rejection, and your own senioritis.

YOU'RE STILL IN CHARGE, BUT THE GAME RULES ARE CHANGING

VOICES OF EXPERIENCE

"It's like pornography: You know it when you see it. The signs are spaciness, inattention to detail, indifference to school work, activities, and family, moodiness, and a certain arrogance—'the rules don't apply to me anymore.'"

Peter Pashler

"With our son, senioritis wasn't about grades. It was more of a personal thing. His goal was to try life in another part of the country. He knew graduation was the jumping-off point, and he knew he was the one responsible for what would happen after that."

Laurie Crawford

"There are two things you need to remember: First, you don't have the privilege of being your child's friend until your child is an adult; second, every child is afraid of making that transition from childhood to adulthood. They still want Mom and Dad to take care of them."

Rich Kelly

The form of government around the house is changing, opening up, and your youngster has more to say about more topics than in the past. Still, "democracy" is not how you'd describe the home scene. It's more like a "benevolent dictatorship" or "participatory autocracy."

Even though your senior has grand illusions about being king of the mountain or queen of the hop, you still must maintain some kind of structure and control at home. This will cause the senior to stomp feet, pout, spend time away from the family, and repeatedly announce that what's going on "IS NOT FAIR!"

To which you will calmly (we hope) point out, "Life is not fair."

You shouldn't, and probably can't, make most of the decisions *for* your child anymore, but when it comes to Big Important Issues, you can make decisions *with* your child.

SUGGESTING TO YOUR CHILD

Suggest that your youngster give herself plenty of alternatives as she continues to take charge of her life. The more doors to the future she can prop open, the more possibilities her future holds. Kids this age don't yet realize that there's always more than one way.

To help your youngster ease into the adult world on a more permanent basis, provide options rather than saying, "You have to do this." Just make sure you can live with the options.

Also, when you're on one side of an issue and your student is on the other, try for a compromise. Just make sure you can live with the compromise.

Through all this turmoil, and in most houses, that's exactly what it is, you don't stop loving the child, but you *do* start to do more loving from a distance.

TRUST

You also have to do a lot of trusting, which is mixed liberally with hope and doubt. That's because you hope your child-turning-adult is always telling you the truth about homework, destinations, drinking, and what friends are doing. But the fact is, you don't know. And that's where the doubt comes in.

Realize that your child may do a lot of things you never know about. One parent talks about feeling comfortable (but not smug—*never* smug) because her son was always in by curfew. It took a very long time before she learned that he was sneaking back out after everyone went to sleep!

If you let the oldest one get away with it (whatever "it" is), you're going to pay for that leniency all the way down the line with younger siblings.

Let your youngster have friends over to spend the night, but unless you know the friends' parents very well, don't let your child spend the night at other peoples' homes.

Wise are the parents who open their home up to their senior student and assorted friends. Having everybody under your roof gives you some control.

VOICES OF EXPERIENCE

"As a rule, in our area boys don't stay overnight with other boys. That's a girl thing. So, if our son said, 'Mom, I'm staying overnight at so-and-so's house tonight,' I'd tell him, 'I don't think so.'"

Laurie Crawford

"We think our kids look so bad, but our son saw a picture of his father wearing a polyester shirt and bell bottoms and big, globby sideburns and he wanted to know who that was!"

Audrey Valhuerdi

HOMEWORK? WHAT HOMEWORK? CURFEW? WHAT CURFEW? (ETC.)

VOICES OF EXPERIENCE

"Our older child was very good at playing the game. He went around to all of his teachers at the end of the first nine weeks of his senior year, explaining how important his grades were to being admitted to college. Our second child received an incomplete in his senior year because he missed a physics test. He was seeking an early admission, and he didn't get in. We think that's why."

Jane Eckstein

"I had senioritis from the time I was a freshman. I didn't even know where the library was my first year of high school. We can't get our daughter out of the library."

Bud Bennett

"Kids need to realize they are not getting good grades for the parents. They're making their own down payment on life. I say to my kids, 'I'll work three jobs to put you through college, but when you're 26 and out of work, it will be your fault, not mine. And the blame will begin with your not doing your work when you were in high school.' "

Rich Kelly

Even though your child is wrapping up the high school career, he still holds control over the choice of senior year courses, the grades earned, the essay, and whom he will ask for letters of recommendation. Not everything is yet set in stone.

Emphasize to your child that each grade for the first semester of senior year must be as good as it gets. Some colleges won't make admissions decisions until they have seen first-semester results. Some require final senior grades and a certification of graduation, and if the grades dropped during senior year, the student may receive a letter asking for an explanation.

Worst case scenario? Some selective schools may reverse their offer of acceptance if the senior grades are low.

Actually, taking difficult courses throughout senior year is excellent preparation for the rigors of university study requirements.

You'll hear the horror stories of kids blowing off senior year, but not every kid feels this compulsion. Yours just may stick to the routine or find a more moderate path.

Two kids from the same family can be *very* different. One is super responsible and the other is pretty much a disaster in that area. That means one set of rules doesn't fit all.

CURFEWS

The biggest control issue may well center around a curfew. It's okay to ask your senior the same question your parents asked you: "What exactly is there to do out there after midnight on a Friday or Saturday night?"

If weekend curfew is midnight, your senior probably will walk in the front door at 12:05. If curfew is 1:00 A.M., she'll show up at 1:05. Worse things could be happening!

If your youngster is the *only kid in the whole world* who has to be in at a certain hour, suggest he invite his friends in to watch a movie.

School nights are different. Plenty of parents expect their seniors to be home studying then, unless they're working or involved in a school activity. (Your kid knows this is the rule in most homes, but it's not information he'll share with you.)

Lucky the parent whose child imposes her own curfew. Usually, it's because she needs the sleep to do well in school or sports.

Some parents say okay to staying out a bit later on a weeknight if their child is part of a study group. (There is an assumption on your part, of course, that the kids are studying.)

The biggie as far as curfew is concerned is prom night. Unless you've been living in a cave, you know the peer pressure for staying out 'til dawn after the prom.

In some communities, that whole prom thing gets out of hand, with expenses that make a credit card melt—from dresses to dinners to limo rides. But the toughest issue may be those hotel rooms after the dance. It's very hard for parents to put the brakes on all of this. Best advice? Work with other parents to set collective parameters. And push for all-night, school-sponsored activities if they don't exist in your community.

Knowing whom your child will be with and where on prom night helps immensely.

Kids who go to prom in groups may have the most fun, and their parents are still sane the next day.

"There were no complaints when I had different curfews for our two kids. After prom, for instance, one went out to a breakfast. I knew the family and was comfortable with the mother, plus I knew the driving situation. So there was no curfew. The other daughter had no plans, so we required her to be in at 2:30 A.M."

Dianne Peterson

"We didn't have that much trouble as far as curfews were concerned. We said, 'You have to be in the house by this hour. After that, the burglar alarm goes on.'"

Audrey Valhuerdi

"Do we have curfews? Absolutely! We have daughters."

Deborah Hafner

PARENT INVOLVEMENT AT SCHOOL—IT'S NOT OVER YET !

"My son started asking me not to be involved in freshmen year, but I got involved anyway. Then, when he moved to a bigger high school and found out there was a PTA, he said, 'Please, Mom, don't go to those meetings!' He did get involved with chess club and I would transport kids and that was okay—for a while."

Audrey Valhuerdi

"I was standing waiting for my car to be washed at a high school fund-raiser. I introduced myself to who I thought was one of my son's teachers, also waiting. We had a nice talk and it made it easier for my son because the teacher saw him as part of a family."

Jennifer Merlin

Not all high schools go out of their way to encourage parents of seniors to get involved, or remain involved, as volunteers. But that doesn't mean you should stay home. Your presence sends a loud-and-clear message to your student that you're still around and you still care.

Do seniors want their parents to be involved? It depends. Being seen with your parent-volunteer is okay if you're together because of band or sports. But your kid does not want you to show up in the classroom or at a German Club meeting.

Students whose parents volunteer for school activities often hear about opportunities simply because the teachers have gotten to know the parent and see the interest in education. It's that squeaky wheel thing.

If you keep in touch with teachers, they are more likely to call you when they have any concern about your youngster, even senior year.

Whether counselors are responsible for 40 or 400 students, knowing you helps them know your senior as an individual who has specific college goals or needs.

By now, you've supplied breakfasts for the swim team at 7:00 A.M., shuttled kids to choral practices, gone to plays, football games, open houses, and conferences, and you're ready to, well, graduate. But like your senior, you've got to hang in there and do good work that whole last year.

Think about it: If you disengage from school your youngster's senior year, he just might do as you do, rather than do as you say.

"We made sure we went to the school's open houses to meet the teachers. This is very important because, even if they don't see you at school the rest of the year, it tells them your child has a support system."

Raquel Johnston

THAT LONG LAST SEMESTER

"It's wonderful when your senior is in a spring sport. Our baseball coach told the players three days before prom that if any of them were going to parties where alcohol was served, or if any of them were thinking of renting motel rooms, they'd be kicked off the team. All of a sudden, there were a lot of moms renting movies."

Cyndi Bennett

> "As far as homework is concerned, I don't think you are going to find a kid who has a good solid sense of responsibility who will quit. They might throttle back a little bit but they won't quit."
>
> Bud Bennett

Many seniors find it very difficult to care about good grades, let alone work for them. And they are given a certain amount of permission to quit since acceptance and rejection letters are mailed throughout senior year. Also, some high schools don't even award second-semester senior grades.

Students react differently to that second-semester grade thing: Student A says, "The college isn't going to know if I goof off second semester, so I think I'll just take it easy. It doesn't really matter." Student B says, "The college may not know if I goof off second semester, but I've worked so hard throughout high school that I want to finish strong." It's easier to be Student B's parent.

The more structured the student, the less likely he is to succumb to senioritis. The stronger the child's study habits, the less likely she is to check out early. And when personal pride is as important to the student as getting admitted to a college, *wow!*

Some students don't take senior grades seriously because they've seen dollar signs in their future, and the jobs aren't connected to a college degree. They know their grades will allow them to graduate, and that's all they care about. They can't envision the door closing on further opportunities about the time they reach 35. (Shoot, they can't even envision 35.)

VOICES OF EXPERIENCE

> "Our high school requires students who are in activities to maintain certain grades. So our kids tried to tell us they were okay grade-wise since they met those requirements. We had to reiterate to them that our expectations were above school expectations. When they were seniors, we said they'd done their job for 11½ years of school, and we expected them to finish what they started!"
>
> Rose Kelly

ACCEPTANCE AND REJECTION

"Our school announces senior awards and scholarships at a program for the whole community. My daughter, fortunately, had been offered four scholarships and we were really proud of her. But when they read her name at the awards program, they only announced the scholarship she had accepted at the college she chose. Afterwards, I asked her how they could have missed the other three, and she replied that she only told them about the one. Our moment of glory and she hadn't told them. But that was the way she did things and it was okay."

Barbara Walker

"Our daughter was the only student in her class who applied to Brown (University) and was not accepted. She was also the only applicant from her school whose dad was not a doctor. I'm not college educated. I figured they were looking beyond the applicants at what may be donated to the college down the road."

Rich Kelly

"I don't see so much stress from getting into a college because the kids know they are going to get in somewhere. I wonder if the stress comes from how much we're expecting of them. I was going to go to a junior college and that was fine with me. Today, there is an underlying theme; it's what the group expects. A kid won't go to a junior college because none of his friends are going there."

John Johnson

With early decision acceptance, all the high drama is over by the mid-December notification.

With early decision rejection, the high drama gets even higher. First, your student has to deal with rejection. (This needs to be discussed ahead of time.) Second, your student will spend the holidays trying to put together applications to other schools. And guess what? Counselors and teachers aren't around then to write recommendations, and registrars aren't around to send transcripts.

Early decision deferral (read that as placement in the regular applications pool) feels a lot like rejection, even though your youngster still may be accepted by that particular college. (This possibility also needs to be discussed ahead of time.) Deferred students also spend the holidays putting together applications to other schools.

Rolling admission notification can come anytime after your completed application reaches the Admissions Office.

With plain ol' regular apps, you get a yea or nay in mid-April. If your youngster gets a little squirrely about that time of year, bear up.

Don't race your student to the mailbox when the notification letters begin to arrive. It's unbecoming. And don't open your kid's mail. Of course, no one said anything about not holding the envelope up to the light . . . .

WAIT-LISTS

Your youngster may get notified that she's wait-listed rather than accepted or rejected. That means the school accepted a certain number of students and is now waiting to see how many of them will say Yes by the May 1 standard response date. Then, the school will invite some who are wait-listed to come on down and fill any vacant slots.

Being wait-listed is good in that your student hasn't yet been told No. It's not so good because you don't know how long he'll have to wait for a Yes or No. As one parent remarked, "Being wait-listed can mean a long time to be put on hold."

Wait-listed students can persist in letting the school know it's their first choice. Maybe they can find out where they are on the list. Maybe they can revisit those schools that have already accepted them to see if they want to reevaluate their first choice.

Visit with the high school counselor for possible help in contacting the college to advocate for your wait-listed youngster. Also, find out what happens with housing options and financial aid possibilities for late-accepted students. Those opportunities may not be the same for wait-listed students, which may help your student adjust his thinking toward another school or even wait a year.

If wait-listed students are ultimately accepted, they probably will have a short time to decide whether to attend that school after all. Wherever your student is accepted, hold your breath until you see the financial aid package, which may not arrive for at least another week.

THUMBS UP

When you know which colleges have accepted your child, the final decision usually shouldn't be based on scholarship or cost alone. Add into the mix the information from The Short, Pretty Serious List of Colleges and your campus visit notes.

Once your child receives acceptance notices, and if the pocketbook isn't already exhausted, send your youngster back to that first-choice school for a weekend by herself. She'll come home with a clear understanding of the attitude and atmosphere of the place, very important factors as she makes a commitment.

For students who are accepted by more than one college, the stress of trying to decide which college to attend may be as bad as the stress of waiting to hear which colleges accepted them.

You can tell your youngster that no decision is final, transferring is an option if the school she picks turns out not to be a good choice, and this will not be the most important decision she'll ever make. But your child probably won't see it like that. She's thinking that if she goes down this road and doesn't make it, her life is lost.

Nobody has a problem with acceptance so your youngster won't have to prepare himself to handle the good news. But before the letters begin to arrive, you may want to talk about the very real possibility that not all of your child's friends will be accepted. If that happens, it's important that your youngster not flaunt his good luck but rather that he be compassionate for a friend who got the thumbs-down sign. Of course, there is also the possibility that your own child will get the thumbs-down sign. And that will be hard to take—for both of you.

Most state universities accept or reject applicants based on objective numbers—GPA and/or test scores. It's different with selective colleges. They put together student bodies that will complement and challenge each other. In other words, colleges look for all kinds of students to create a good learning environment. If the school needs a cellist and your kid plays soccer, the school will probably take the cellist, even if your soccer player's SAT score was 1500 and the cellist's score was 1400. If your child is rejected, it may be because the match wasn't right at this particular moment in the history of the world.

THUMBS DOWN

Urge your child not to take any rejection personally. (The same goes for you.) Also, try really hard to remember that if your student doesn't get into a particular school, the rest of his life will not be ruined. Nor will yours.

When the time is right, discuss options. There are always options, although you may want to enlist your guidance counselor's help to find them. Your youngster could take a year off, doing something to bolster her confidence before reapplying (see "I Wanna Wait a Year!," page 181). She could attend a second-choice school or community college for a semester or year and then reapply with a showing of good college grades. She could cry (and well she may). She could also appeal the rejection, although appealing is very rare.

Remember, whether it's acceptance or rejection, this is still your child's news to tell classmates, friends, and relatives.

Have your child send notes to those schools that offered acceptance letters but were not your student's final choice. Thank the schools for the acceptance and explain why the offer was declined. A thank you is—plain and simple—courteous, and down the road, your kid could end up reapplying there.

"There's an attitude about community colleges and state schools. It's true with both peers and parents. People come up to you and say, 'Where does your child go college?' and if it isn't some big-name school, it's almost like you are embarrassed to say."

Jerry Rewa

"If your child is rejected by a college, he may not talk about it, but you'll know. After my son got a rejection notice, he took the dog for a long walk. He came back home, threw the leash down, and said, 'Don't touch me. I'm leaving.' I knew what had come in that day's mail."

Gail Walzer

ANXIETY AS AN ART FORM—STUDENTS FROM HELL

"Seniors accumulate many half-truths. As I listened to all the kids, I'd hear statements that would make very good sense statistically for a whole entering class at one institution, but the kids were using the information indiscriminately. They would make a statement that was true about a school they were talking about, but then they would generalize that idea to all schools. That way their information became almost like gossip—it was certainly true for some situations, but not in general."

Gene Eckstein

"It's kind of like sex—they say they know all about it but they don't, really."

Susie Polden

"Our child went through all kinds of hair colors and haircuts from one month to the next. I asked him to please grow his hair until his graduation pictures were taken. I said he'd look at that picture in 20 years and say, 'My God, why didn't somebody tell me?' Then, I said, 'Well, I'm telling you now.'"

Jennifer Merlin

"You want to believe what your children tell you, but it's scary. They're going to go to college, they're going to be away from us, and they're going to experiment. I know they will do that because that is what we did."

Jim Evans

First, the senior thinks about how high school is almost over, and feels relief. Then, the senior thinks about the ensuing summer of freedom, and feels joy. Then, the senior thinks about leaving home, and feels hollow. Then, the senior thinks about starting college, and feels scared . . . .

In the fall of the senior year, kids believe they see the light at the end of the tunnel. Come springtime, they find out what they're looking at is the front end of a train. This causes a fairly emotional reaction.

A major problem with the high school senior is that he really isn't a child anymore. Then again, he really isn't an adult, either. This produces anxiety for the child-adult—or the adult-child. It all depends upon the day.

Realize that there are now certain areas of your child's life over which you no longer have control. (You know this won't be easy, don't you?)

When you start to tiptoe around those certain areas, think twice before asking a question or offering an unsolicited opinion. You may not care for your child's response but the only thing you can do about that response is— nothing. And that's another shocker.

Whether they realize it or not, seniors are trying to detach from the family. They know there's this major separation coming up in the fall, and they're getting ready. Or, are they getting you ready?

That looming detachment causes them to do strange things. Suddenly, they'll just get up and walk away from the dinner table, angry over something you didn't even know was controversial. Much of the time, they're simply working themselves up to that break with the family. It may not be how *you* would make the break, but then, you aren't a high school senior.

"We had one child who was willing to work hard to earn certain privileges at home and another who wasn't. Now, the one who didn't get those privileges is griping about what his brother gets. I just tell him he could have had those privileges and perks, but he insisted on throwing them out the window. That took care of the comments."

Audrey Valhuerdi

"There's a period of time between application and acceptance or rejection—you don't hear from anybody. Our daughter had always wanted Berkeley and she couldn't stand the stress of waiting. I'd say, 'You have other places to go if you don't get in,' and, 'We love you anyway.' But that didn't help. Her group of friends would dash home every noon to get the mail, but then they'd be afraid to talk to each other because one might have received something and nobody else did."

Kathy Hafner

ANXIETY AS AN ART FORM— PARENTS AREN'T EXEMPT

"Once I told (my wife) Rose to go to her room. I gave her a time-out. The kids loved it."

Rich Kelly

"Be careful what threats you make because you must follow through on them."

Jerry Crawford

"My daughters and I had the big sex talks while we were driving eight hours to Tallahassee. You can't go anywhere when you're in a car. One daughter was immediately unwilling to listen; the other would allow me to talk. There is a difference. We never talked much about drugs because the girls got so much information at school."

Dianne Peterson

"Before they get their driver's license and are out by themselves, talk with them several times about drugs and alcohol. Once they get their license and are more independent, they're going to do what they're going to do about those things."

Michael Johnston

A major cause of parent anxiety is the realization that you no longer serve as a buffer between your child and the worldly realities of drinking, drugs, and sex.

Even though your kid doesn't want to talk to you about those issues, *and* even though you don't want to talk about them, either, they're important and must be discussed.

Hopefully, these senior-level discussions won't be the first ones you've had. But because your youngster is assuming increasing responsibility for himself, you owe him the benefit of your wisdom.

So, what can you say to somebody entering the adult world, but not yet quite through the door? Every parent has a different take on this, but the collective message we heard is:

A. If you are going to drink—and we hope you won't—use moderation and have a designated driver. If there's no designated driver, call home and let us know where you are.
B. Don't do drugs. *Ever*. Period.
C. If you are going to have sex—and we hope you won't—use a condom.

DRINKING

- Some parents think it's okay to have a beer with their underage youngster and his peers. Other parents aren't around to even know their youngster and her peers are drinking. Still other parents consistently tell the kids they don't condone underage drinking. But if the kids know of anyone drinking, the parents say, urge them to always have a designated driver.

- Keep your questions about drinking general, so you don't back your youngster into a corner. Instead of saying, "Were you drinking at the party last night?" try asking, "Was there a lot of drinking at the party last night?" The former sounds accusatory. The latter provides an opportunity to talk.

- Some parents say, " 'Fess up." If you did your share of drinking when you were young, tell your youngster, but don't brag about it. Kids appreciate knowing that their parents weren't perfect. Other parents say, "Never confess."

ILLEGAL DRUGS

- Your child already knows that drugs aren't good for him. But what he may not realize is that drugs can ruin a career long after the user has stopped doing drugs. That's not something our invincible teenagers think about.

178

- Tell kids to be cognizant of where they are and whom they are with. It's the birds of a feather flock together thing. If one kid has drugs, it's likely the other kids with him will also be arrested.

- If your child ends up with a roommate who does drugs, encourage your youngster to meet with the RA. Even if your own student doesn't do drugs, she can end up paying for that association for a long time to come.

SEX

- Young adults often don't acknowledge the physical hazards of engaging in sexual activity. They do not believe they will contract an infection, least of all a life-threatening one. Nor do they contemplate pregnancy. Stuff like that happens to somebody else.

- These youngsters also don't realize the mental hazards of engaging in sexual activity. They think passion, attention, and security. Often, they get guilt, fear, jealousy, loss of self-esteem, anger—the works.

- While we're at it, they don't always understand that sex changes a relationship, either. You can be going with someone and have a nice relationship, but once sex is involved, the relationship often changes.

You've probably noticed high school kids see no shades of gray in any situation. It's only good or bad. For example, if your youngster is antidrinking and there is liquor at a party, it's a bad party. If someone takes a drink, that's a bad person. Most college students don't have that good-bad attitude, which can make adjustment difficult for those who do.

It's a given that the kid's senioritis will cause you anxiety. While there's no cure, parents have offered a few Band-Aids:

- Cry, but not at the grocery store or at work.

- Talk with your child. Or, to be on the safe side, let the kid talk and you listen. Periodically, nod and say, "Ah, yes," and "I see." File away your opinions most of the time.

- Let your youngster pick the topic of conversation. Then, try not to sound like the parent of a senior. That can terminate conversations very quickly.

- Go to your room. This is easier than sending the senior to her room; plus if there's a good book on your nightstand, reading is a great way to get beyond the moment.

- Invite your senior out, to a movie or a ballgame. However, for many kids this age, being seen with a parent at any public spot besides a restaurant is, quite frankly, mortifying.

- Spend some time alone with your younger children. They probably still like you a lot.

- Ask friends who also have seniors what's going on at their house. It's always reassuring to know you aren't the only one paddling the boat around in circles.
- If you're a two-parent family, remember to support one another.
- If you're a single parent, seek the advice and support of a caring, respected friend of the opposite sex, someone who can help you see the whole picture by adding a perspective it may be impossible for you to have.
- Do not go up to the parents of a darling two-year-old and say, "Just wait! Just you wait!"
- Realize that in five years, or even less, your youngster will note that you've become smarter, more enjoyable to be with, and, occasionally, an interesting conversationalist. You may sometimes be clever but probably never actually funny. And being seen with you in public will no longer mortify your child.
- One more thing: When you do go out in public with your adult-kid down the road, still bring the plastic.

VOICES OF EXPERIENCE

"We told our son to be cognizant of where you are and who you are with. If you're in the wrong place at the wrong time with the wrong group, you can be counted as part of the trouble."

Michael Merlin

"I told him, 'They'll take you first with that Mohawk (haircut) and all kinds of odd dress and gear, the belts, lace-up boots . . . .'"

Jennifer Merlin

"As far as drinking is concerned, don't give them permission to try. Tell them, 'It's not okay with me.'"

Kathy Hafner

"Let kids know the options. A designated driver is one of them. That term just wasn't around when we were in college. The last one in the car drove. We didn't have seat belts, then, or baby car seats. There are a lot of changes."

Nancy Johnson

"I WANNA WAIT A YEAR!"

VOICES OF EXPERIENCE

"Our daughter took a year off before going to college. She lived with relatives in Germany and took twelfth grade again. That really helped her get a sense of herself. By the time she went to college, she was totally empowered. If a student doesn't know who she is and where she is going, there is no reason to rush into college. Especially if there are possibilities to explore."

Mary Doll

Some seniors decide that college can wait a year. This can happen before or even after letters of acceptance have arrived. The mere mention of postponing college causes parents to gulp Maalox. Better to relax; the notion is most likely the result of jitters. Reassure your child that she is ready for the college experience.

Still, don't totally rule out the possibility of taking time off between high school and college. Every person is different and some may need another year to mature or to figure out what they want out of a college education. Best advice? Listen to what your child is saying. Kids this age often know themselves better than we think.

If your youngster is insistent at this late date that he wants to sit out a year, it is time for some serious talks about money. That will be a huge factor.

OTHER ACTIVITIES BESIDES COLLEGE

If, in the end, the year off gets the green light, make sure it counts for something. There are a zillion ways a kid might spend the time productively rather than flipping burgers and raiding the fridge. For starters, your youngster might:

—globe-hop from being an *au pair* in the Swiss Alps to working on a *kibbutz* in Israel;
—assist in a daycare center (potential education majors);
—work in a community health center (potential doctors or nurses);
—take classes, especially in creative areas like dance, art, writing, or fixing motors;
—play for a sports team;
—become fluent in a foreign language by living abroad;

—work for a wilderness adventure company to learn leadership and survival skills;

—go through a thirteenth year of school as a postgraduate to learn stuff that slipped through the cracks the previous twelve years.

Such "time off" experiences enrich and inform. They may even do as much to help your student develop a love of lifelong learning with college as the big kick-off event the next year.

Our parents' generation would have viewed taking a year off as unthinkable. There was an unspoken fear that a child who took a year off would never go to college at all. But today, lots of students take a year off, and most do go on to college.

What about those who don't want to go now, or ever? First, realize that it's their life and their choice. And know that there are people who have a good strong work ethic and no college degree as well as those who have a degree but no work ethic.

Look around you. Not everyone needs a college degree to succeed. After all, Bill Gates dropped out and never went back. (Maybe that's not something you should tell your student!)

"For students who really don't want to go to college, it cuts down on the stress if you talk about college as one option, a place to get more skills. Suggest they may not want to close that door yet. Tell them that while they may not use that degree, they'll probably use the experience they gain in college."

Nancy Johnson

CHAPTER 10

LEAVING HOME— SLOWLY, IT SUDDENLY HAPPENS

They can't wait to go away, but they don't pack, either. Here's how to survive the long, hot, beyond-senior summer while keeping your cool. Included are tips about freshman classes and orientation, what to take, who should pack, calling new roommates, transporting the youngster to campus and, finally, saying good-bye.

GRADUATION AND THE ENDLESS SUMMER

VOICES OF EXPERIENCE

"That summer I started thinking of our daughter as 'the drape.' She was constantly leaning on us, just clinging. It was literally weight on our bodies. She quit the clinging when she left for school, but that whole first year of college, she was very tactile."

Mary Doll

"Then, there was our son. He was ready to leave by eleventh grade. He said no way were we going to take him to college, that he'd fly out on his own. In fact, he was so anxious to be gone that when he finally got on the plane, my wife and I gave each other high fives at the gate."

Henry C. Doll

"Our youngest was a girl. When it was time for her to go to college, her two older brothers' only piece of advice was: Never tell the parents anything."

Jim Adams

Inexperienced parent: I've never had a child go through this endless-summer thing before. Do you think my kid will be kind of grumpy?

Experienced parent: Ha Ha Ha Ha Ha Ha Ha Ha!!!!

Since your youngster is already preparing for a life-altering experience (let's face it, that's what college is), this might not be the best summer to sell the house, trade cars, and get a dog. Or get rid of a dog. And for goodness sake, don't talk about how you'll redecorate the graduate's bedroom come fall!

Measure your words about what life around the homestead will be like once the graduate is out the door. Too much "Woe is me!" on your part can make a child feel guilty about leaving. And too much "Wow! No more daily parenting!" can make a child feel unwanted at home.

College-bound youngsters slip into all sorts of roles:

- Some seem so excited about leaving for college that they can barely stand it. Others appear completely nonchalant. Don't take either approach at face value. The summer before independence can be the most insecure summer of a young life.

- Some sail through the summer. For them, getting ready for college will be just like getting ready for camp, except they'll be packing more clothes.

- Some turn the household into a trauma center. They may be overly apprehensive about leaving home, or they may be hell-bent to get out of there. They're the ones who claim loudly that it's time for them to do their own thing, if only they knew what their thing was. Whichever scenario plays out at your house, high drama results.

- Some go through the entire summer, barely uttering a word. Others dump 18 years' worth of problems on your head, first in June, then in July, and again in August. Whether your youngster is silent or constantly chattering, work at communication. Over and over and over. Every single day.

No matter which category (or categories) your youngster slips into, you don't need to mention that the first semester of college almost always is tough. The old network of friends has disappeared and your child has to start over again, usually in a bigger pond.

Encourage your student to have a busy, productive summer. That should keep boredom, or even worse, depression, at bay.

Perhaps the biggest challenge of the endless summer is realizing that your child is actually a young adult. So remember, if she decides to tell you something, she probably means, "I'm telling you what I'm going to do," rather than, "I'm asking you what to do." Big difference!

There may be times, though, when your child means, "I'm telling you what I'm going to do," but means, "I'm asking you what to do." So how do you know one situation from the other? Good question.

Most of the time, you can take off your problem-solver hat and put on your good-listener hat. Both fit fine, but the problem-solver hat still feels more comfortable.

There is a part of you that expects the future to be absolutely terrific. After all, you're about to launch your child into a fantastic future and how could everything not be wonderful! Well, guess what . . . .

The fact is, you cannot guarantee your child will be happy down the road, so you need to say, "Let's talk" now. Talk about strategies for coping. Talk about feelings. Talk about why it's okay to make mistakes. Talk about how the door will always be open and you'll always be there. Then always be there.

If you're half of a two-parent family, don't forget about your other half right now. Difficult times put dents in a marriage.

If you're a single parent, be honest with your youngster when you need some breathing space, and then take it, whether it's five minutes or two hours. Wonderful bosses also can be a boon to single parents, allowing them to take time to go to college orientation and other activities.

THE THINGS-TO-DO LIST

For the things-to-do list: Make an appointment for your daughter with a gynecologist. She may think that's the dumbest idea you've ever had, but she's wrong. Neither you nor she knows what may happen and this meeting will provide her with a responsible adult in whom she can confide, if the need arises.

Now, if you make that appointment and your daughter absolutely, positively, emphatically, vehemently, and unilaterally refuses to go, cancel the appointment. Then sigh and consider talking with her yourself about Acquired Immune Deficiency Syndrome (AIDS), Sexually Transmitted Diseases (STDs), date rape—all the sex things you hope she'll never encounter because she's well informed.

And it's not just the girls who need a medical connection. Send your boys to an internist or family practitioner. Guys, too, need someone to talk with them about AIDS, STDs, date rape, responsible sex, and abstinence. The world can get crazy out there!

Also, while all institutions have some kind of health center, for the cough that won't give up or for serious illnesses or injuries that might occur at school, these visits now will ensure that your young adult has a doctor all set up at home base if you want another opinion.

Does all this sex talk make you squirm a bit? Realize that in most dorms today, men and women live on the same floor and share bathrooms where birth control information is posted on the walls.

If you haven't yet stopped "doing" for your child, get out the scissors and start working on those apron strings. After all, your youngster will be leaving home in August or September, and then you can't "do," even if you want to.

VOICES OF
EXPERIENCE

"Baby boomer parents have always been so involved in their child's life. We started that with the PTA and we just kept going. It can be carried over to college campus, you know, where you see parents arriving to work out class schedules."

Joyce Batipps

"We had a talk with our son that summer about how he should never allow himself to be put in a position where he could be accused of date rape. We told him we were sure he wouldn't do anything like that, but he needed to protect himself. Kids can be accused of things they are not guilty of."

Karen Dakin

ORIENTATION AND CHOOSING CLASSES

VOICES OF EXPERIENCE

"During orientation, they talked a lot about ethnicity on campus. Plus, all of the ethnic groups and organizations put on a show. They introduced themselves and talked to us about the whole racial thing. I'm Hispanic, and I have to say I left that day feeling good."

Sheila Ayala

"At orientation, the food service supervisor told all of us parents, 'Call me if your child doesn't call home. I see the kid three times a day and I'll have him call you.'"

Chris Sweeney

"We went to a two-day orientation for freshmen and besides the tour, it was absolutely no help at all. We received very little information. So when we got back home, I started making phone calls. I called the admissions office. I called the financial aid office. I talked to anybody who would listen until I got my answers."

Audrey Valhuerdi

Every school makes up its own orientation schedule for incoming students. Thus, orientation may be in the spring, summer, or just before school begins. It may be a day, a week, or a weekend.

If you're invited to orientation activities, and if you have the time and money to go, treat the event as a short vacation. It will be different—and halfway relaxing. Also, you'll get lots of information your youngster won't give you himself because it isn't important to him.

Or, you may be invited to nothing at all. Not every school has orientation activities for parents. Maybe they're cutting the cord for you.

At some mid-summer orientations, students register for classes, see where they'll live (but can't move in, no matter how ready you both are), find out how to use their meal plan card, take placement tests for classes, and go to dorm meetings and social activities. It's busy, but it helps your student begin to feel comfortable on campus before the big break from home occurs. The same things happen at orientations held just before school starts, but then your youngster can move in.

WHAT SCHOOL OFFICIALS DISCUSS AT ORIENTATIONS

School officials discuss how you can support your child from a distance. They also talk about what you should expect of them while your child is under their roof. (That's also when officials might broach that five-year-program thing, the one every parent is convinced will not happen to their child.)

They should address everything you ever wanted to know and then some: sex; crime; campus security and safety; counseling and testing services; drugs and alcohol; unique job opportunities for students; and companies that bake and deliver cakes for students' birthdays or provide stress-buster packages during exam week.

Somewhere in there, they may tell you that your A-student likely will not score straight As in college. In fact, success in many classes may just mean passing with a C. One more tidbit: Students probably receive their lowest grades during—you guessed it—freshman year.

Administrators will talk about college organizations and activities and try to give you a sense of life on campus. But realize that they, like parents, may not always know *everything* that is going on. Negative issues such as fraternity hazing can crop up later and the reason you weren't "warned" may be because the administrators themselves didn't know.

You'll probably hear all about the college's high graduation rate, but administrators may not tell you about coed bathrooms or visitation rights. And chances are, your student won't mention those issues, either.

OTHER PARTS OF ORIENTATION

If orientation includes a family dinner or picnic, you'll be able to spot the parents of freshmen boys. They're the adults who don't have any kids eating with them.

Some colleges pair upperclassmen with freshmen at orientation to help with the adjustments, homework, and whatever else comes along. For parents and new students, that big brother/big sister approach is very reassuring.

If your soon-to-be freshman gets invited by a school-sponsored club to go hiking, biking, or something mildly adventuresome just before classes begin, tell her it's a great way to meet other students. Then she won't have to sit by herself in the cafeteria. Remind her, however, that finding a best friend or two comes later.

Your child is already savoring the fact that he'll no longer be living with parents who say things like, "Now, dear, remember our rules . . . ." So remind him to check the college's rules for class sign-up, registration deadlines, fees for late registration, fees for late drop and add classes, requirements for declaring a major, classes required for that major—and on and on and on. This could make those home rules look easy!

And for goodness' sake, make sure he carefully reads each course's content in the school catalog. Spanish III may be the third year of Spanish language, or it could be a study of the history of Spain. Big difference if your student just wants to become fluent in Spanish.

SURPRISES FOR PARENTS

Here's a surprise for some parents: Many institutions send kids' grades to them, not the parents. You could go four years and not have a clue about what your youngster really studied, or didn't study, as grades might show.

Here's another surprise: Some colleges won't release any medical information about your child unless she's signed a release.

And here's some good news about those surprises: At some schools, students can sign forms requesting that grades and/or medical information be sent to you. Orientation is a good time to discuss how much information you'd like. Depending upon your decision, have your youngster sign the forms while you're still on campus.

VOICES OF EXPERIENCE

"I visited my daughter her first semester of college. It was an all-girls school, but boys could visit in the dorms one weekend a month. I went into the bathroom and there was a guy in the shower. I screamed and ran out. The school didn't tell us about that at orientation."

Sheila Ayala

"One college sent a letter telling us that our child would be different when he returned home after being at school for a while. The letter encouraged conversation between us so the growth would not become a negative focus but rather a source of joy."

Gene Eckstein

"Three years ago when our first son went off to college, people said we didn't need to go to orientation because he was a young adult. I disagreed. The college students helping with orientation step out of their 'orientation shirts' and tell you what life on campus is really like. We have another son going to college next year and we're going to orientation again because so much has changed."

Jennifer Merlin

GOING GREEK

"I encouraged our daughter to pledge a sorority because I thought sororities had evolved since the sixties. I had an image of bright, young women teaching networking skills to other women. The letters home weren't about mentoring. Much to my chagrin, I found out that girls were still getting points for running around stealing guys' pictures off a fraternity house wall."

Joyce Pope

"Often, invitations to join a sorority or fraternity are issued after having spent very little time with a person. When our daughter was deciding that she wanted to join a particular sorority, she asked how she was going to feel next year when it came time to choose who would get in based on knowing somebody for five hours."

Maricel York

"I was Greek and had a great experience. But when it was time for my son to go to college, I didn't encourage or discourage him from going Greek. Then, he called and said he was interested in a fraternity. When I found out it wasn't mine, I about croaked. I called national and told them to get somebody over on that campus to talk to him. He was in a dorm with 1,300 freshmen that was like a mini-city. In the end, he and his two roommates did join the 'other' fraternity. Since then, I've watched him interact with others and I think his social skills have improved. Maybe it was the fraternity and maybe it was the college experience."

Joe Kirsch

"We didn't do Greek in the sixties. In fact, we marched against them. So when our girls went off to college, they had no intentions of going Greek. Then, at the beginning of her junior year, our oldest called home and said, 'Now, Mom, don't laugh, but I'm going to join a sorority.' I laughed—I didn't mean to, but I thought she was kidding. She said, 'It's the group of people and the sorority I want to spend my time with.' Those are the girls she still stays in contact with."

Kathy Hafner

To be or not to be—Greek—is the question for many incoming fresh-men. If your child is thinking Greek this summer, talk about the pluses and minuses before he leaves for college.

Certainly, one of the minuses is deciding to pledge, then not being in-vited to join. The rejection can be harsh, and, unfortunately, it comes at a time in your child's life when everything he's ever known is changing. It's a given that your child will be able take Yes for an answer at the end of rush. It's imperative that he also be able to accept No.

Explain that during rush, students gravitate toward people just like themselves, which is fine. But also discuss how important it will be to have a variety of friends on campus, some Greek and some non-Greek, some like you and some different. That's one of the richest experiences the college campus offers.

Remind your child, too, that some of the greatest lessons to be learned in college will come not from textbooks, but from the people with whom she rubs elbows. The more diverse the elbows, the richer the experience.

Just because an older sibling is Greek is not a valid reason for a younger one to pledge. Just because the parents or grandparents went Greek is also not a valid reason for the child/grandchild to pledge. If your youngster says, "No way," try to remember which one of you actually would be doing the pledge chores and going to all the meetings and parties.

Legacies are students whose close relative is an alum of a Greek organi-zation in college. Being a legacy may carry some advantage, such as the Greek house having more information about the legacy before rush begins.

Individual Greek houses and the Greek system on individual campuses change constantly. If your youngster is looking at a particular sorority or fraternity on a particular campus, and if you know someone whose child was part of that system in the fairly recent past, talk to that parent. Their stu-dent's experiences and insights may be helpful, whether or not your young-ster actually pledges.

During rush, encourage your child to talk with under- as well as upper-classmen in the fraternity or sorority. After all, the seniors will only be around for one more year. (At least, that's what their parents hope.)

UPS AND DOWNS OF THE GREEK SYSTEM

- Example: The Greek system provides an opportunity to learn leadership and social skills without gender complications. Still, the lessons may be expensive. Greeks can be nickeled and dimed to death by dues, special collections, proj-ects, and functions. Or hit big time if the chapter is redecorating the house.

- Example: Freshman year is difficult. Being part of a Greek system can give structure to students' lives and provide a close circle of friends that may be more difficult to find in a dorm filled with a thousand other kids. But the familial aspects of a sorority or fraternity that at first are comforting may later become structural confines once students find their own legs.

- Example: Many houses have mandatory study hours. But some houses also suggest what members might wear to a party or what activities they might consider joining. (At least that's what students are telling the parents back home.)

In the end, advising your youngster whether or not to go Greek comes back to knowing your child and knowing the fit. If your child wants the camaraderie of a Greek system without being in it, suggest looking into a service organization, student government, or a club sport.

"Our son called and said he was moving into a fraternity house the next day and that he wouldn't be in touch with us for a week. We were unhappy. We'd heard tales of hazing and initiations from friends with students on other campuses. Finally, that next Sunday, we called him. He said, 'It's over. It was the worst week of my life,' and he wouldn't ever say anymore about it."

Joe Kirsch

"My daughter was accepted into a high school form of Greek life but saw other girls emotionally abused by it. So when she went to college, she stereotyped it, thinking it was nothing more than debutantes. But in her junior year, she zeroed in on the right sorority, one that was into volunteering, not materialistic. She went on to become the chapter president."

Jacquie Evans

HIDE THE PLASTIC—CLOTHES DON'T MAKE THE FRESHMAN

"Our son put more time and energy into selecting the right stereo than buying clothes."

Wally Gingerich

Kids usually don't have a clue what kind of clothes they'll need until they get to campus and see what everyone else is wearing. Better to ride out the advertising waves of summer and then take a look-see on campus before shopping.

If the shopping bug bites before you leave home, pick up storage stacking units and school and drugstore supplies instead of new clothes. Your student will be able to rack up a year's worth of personal supplies on your credit card, and then, amazingly, he will be able to do it again the first time he comes home for a visit.

If you skipped the discussion in Chapter 4 about computers, flip back to that section to see what parents say about buying computers. In a nutshell, see what kind of computer and printer the college recommends. Then, if your pocketbook can afford it, buy both for your college-bound student.

It's not like the old days: CD players, VCRs, TVs, refrigerators, microwaves, fans, and rugs are common in today's dorm rooms. But don't whip out that plastic until your child has touched base with the roommate-stranger about who's responsible for what. Also, some schools rent some of those big-ticket items. But comparison shop because it may be less expensive to buy than to rent. And sometimes, large discount stores provide shuttle buses from campus to store and back during move-in days.

Even more to pack:

- You can send along an ironing board, vacuum, mop, and cleaning supplies but don't ask your child if they are ever used. The answer will cause you to hold your head, rock back and forth, and moan, "That is not how this kid was raised!"
- Will your child need a humidifier? Or an air purifier for allergies?
- If the dorm room walls are cement block or cinder block, purchase some putty to put up posters (still a necessary part of life).
- You can buy envelopes, address them to yourself, and affix stamps, but the only letters you're likely to receive are ones that say, "Please send money."
- Do the dorm beds require standard or extra-long fitted sheets? If you purchase the weekly laundry service, do you think your youngster actually will go drop off and pick up clean sheets? And then make the bed? Speaking of sheets, one student bought 10 fitted sheets and put them all on at once. We hate to tell you this, but when the top sheet got dirty, he simply pulled it off and threw it away. Lest you think such shabby treatment of sheets is a guy thing, we know a coed who didn't always have time to wash her sheets, so she vacuumed them.

TOUCHING BASE WITH THE ROOMMATE-STRANGER

VOICES OF EXPERIENCE

"It was very interesting to watch our son and his two roommates get settled in their dorm room. One roommate brought linens and a comforter—all color-coordinated—and made his bed they way they do in the Army. The second put on the fitted sheet and pillowcases and called it a day. The third one didn't bring sheets to college."

Dennis Rhodes

Colleges usually send questionnaires to incoming freshmen in an attempt to make good roommate matches. They'll ask your child about rooming with a smoker, about a preference for staying up late or getting up early, and about decibel tolerance on the CD player.

It's hard for a neat-freak student to room with one who's never met messes he didn't like. Even if that issue isn't addressed in the questionnaire, encourage your youngster to indicate to the college which type of roommate he'll be. (FYI, if he's neat now, he'll still be neat in the dorm. If he's a disaster now, dorm life will not fix that.)

The questionnaire may not address the only-child/sibling issue, but common sense says there are bound to be adjustments when one roommate is an only child and the other has siblings, especially if that sibling grew up sharing a bedroom.

Brace yourself. Your youngster may be asked if she would mind her roommate's boyfriend staying all night. This could generate some interesting family discussions, but do remember to whom the questionnaire was addressed in the first place.

Along with that thought, you could tell your youngster you won't read what he writes on his roommate and health center forms unless he asks you to, but you can still discuss any thoughts or respond to questions he may have.

ROOMING WITH A HIGH SCHOOL FRIEND

Encourage discussion if your child decides to room with a high school friend. Young persons don't understand that absence *does* make the heart grow fonder. For example:

- If your daughter lives with her friend, she'll find out things about her she didn't necessarily want to know.

- Now she probably overlooks some of her friend's irritating little habits like knuckle cracking. But once they're living together, those habits can become fodder for nasty conversations.

- She won't meet as many new people as she would if she were striking out on her own.

TOUCHING BASE WITH THE ROOMMATE BEFOREHAND

Touching base during the summer with the roommate-stranger guarantees your youngster knows the name of at least one person before arriving on campus. And that can slide the meter way up on the comfort scale (your scale as well as your child's).

Knowing a bit about the freshman roommate before meeting the roommate doesn't guarantee a fit, but it does guarantee a start that is a bit less strained.

During the summer, most roommate-strangers will talk to each other about bedspreads and microwaves and printers. They probably won't talk to each other about having opposite-sex overnight guests.

When problems occur (and they will), your child probably will work them out alone. If that doesn't work, most colleges have a procedure for mediating problems through the residence hall advisor.

VOICES OF EXPERIENCE

"Our daughter's roommate's boyfriend moved into the girls' very small room in October of freshman year. We didn't know anything about it for three months. Once our daughter shared the information, she and her dad figured out an alternative. Actually, she announced what she was going to do and was looking for our support. I was glad it got worked out, but what bothered me was her tolerating it for so long because she didn't want to offend anyone."

Karen Dakin

"Our son's roommate made two international calls home at $130 apiece on our son's phone. When our son got the bill, he called home and asked what we were going to do about it. I said, 'It's your roommate; you handle it.' So, first our son confronted the roommate, who denied making the calls. Next, our son went to his residence hall advisor, who also said the roommates needed to work it out. So, finally, our son went back to the roommate and said, 'Listen, you better pay that phone bill. You don't want my mother to come down here and handle this!' The roommate paid the bill in full."

Paula Dawson

"I HAVE TO TAKE MY LETTER JACKET, ALL MY STUFFED ANIMALS, A TV . . ."

> "Kids want to take everything they own with them. It's like they're moving out and never coming back. Our son played hockey in high school, and he wanted to take all his hockey stuff with him to college, even though he was going to be in a warm climate, attending a school that had no hockey program."
>
> **Cathy Sweeney**

At some point during the endless summer, the college should provide your student with a list of items to bring, and not to bring. For example, most colleges don't allow students to have halogen lamps or hot plates because of a potential fire.

Encourage your child to keep his own running list of items to take as well: one column should be for items the new freshman will *Need;* the other column should be for items the new freshman will *Want.*

You may not always agree with your child's placement of items under the Needs column versus the Wants column. For example, you think a new car should be in the Wants column, whereas your child *knows* a new car goes in the Needs column. This will lead to a parent-child conversation.

Once the Needs and Wants are determined, encourage your youngster to consult with the roommate-stranger about who's bringing what; otherwise, the kids can end up with two microwaves and no refrigerator.

Students probably should do their own packing. But often, mothers do it because:

A. They value neatness.
B. They're recalling every mistake they ever made in their child's first 18 years and they're going for forgiveness.
C. They still want to retain a bit of control.
D. Any or all of the above.

PACKING

Some kids pack their belongings neatly into suitcases, boxes, and/or trunks. Others stuff everything into really big backpacks and trombone cases. If your child falls into the latter category, remember that you don't have to watch the unpacking process.

Don't forget a good security lock for the bicycle. (Your bike rider did check on storage space, right?)

Stick in a roll of dimes and quarters for the washer and dryer. Your kid will *never* think to do that!

Promise you won't throw away what she leaves behind. Then don't, even if you believe she won't miss that ratty T-shirt from seventh grade soccer.

"I purchased six see-through containers and put labels on each one. Socks. Underwear. You know. When the containers came back at the end of freshman year, they had stuff in them like dirty pillowcases and homework."

Sheila Ayala

GETTING THERE—STOPPING TO SEE AUNT MARGARET ON THE WAY

"We were supposed to leave home at eight o'clock in the morning. When we finally got all packed, it was 7:00 P.M. So that was 'our trip.'"

Cathy Sweeney

If you're like some families, you'll make the trip to school a rolling party. Stop to see family and friends, ride the *Maid of the Mist* under Niagara Falls, or stroll down the Riverwalk in San Antonio. Pass by the hamburger joints and go for a taste of Thailand. At night, forgo TV in the motel room and play cards instead. Savor your time together!

If you know what still needs to be purchased, throw in a shopping spree along the way. Nothing plugs a kid in more than spending the parents' money!

If you're like other families, the journey to campus will be the trip from Hell. If that's the case, don't prolong the anxiety with visits to Aunt Margaret who will only ask, "Whatayawanna major in?"

Even when fun abounds, the journey will be stressful. After all, you'll be returning home without this child you've been raising for 18 years. The stress can be even greater if you have other children at home to get ready for school, or if taking time off to make the trip is putting you way behind in your own job.

Taking your child to school means you can see the dorm room, take the roommate-stranger out to eat, and meet the residence hall advisor. Once back home, envisioning your youngster in the new setting will mean the world to you.

Bringing younger siblings along also helps them later on to picture Big Brother or Big Sister on campus. They need that visual connection as much as you do

Some parents take photos of the new nest, before it gets that lived-in look.

If you put your child on the big airplane alone, there will be a lot of crying in the airport. Once the plane is airborne, however, you'll feel better. (Well, a little better.)

"Our son was so anxious to leave that it was, like, just get in the car and let's go. I asked him what he wanted to do about his clothes and he said he'd send for them later."

Chris Sweeney

SAYING GOOD-BYE—WHO'S CRYING NOW?

"When we went to college, my brother and I packed our clothes into the car and drove three states away. Our parents were never emotional or expressive about what was happening. That is still etched in my mind. I worried that when my own kids were leaving for college, we, too, might be so busy being traditional parents that we wouldn't think about how the experience was for our children. Or about how they perceived us. Parents should share with their children how they are feeling."

Wally Gingerich

"We were on campus all day, moving in, arranging the room, and all that. I recall wondering how long I would last without crying and did really well until the dinner and speeches. The walk back to the dorm was very long and we suddenly didn't seem to have anything to say. There was a sense of wanting to get the leaving over, but not wanting the moment to come. When it did, it was over very fast. Our child was certainly ready for us to leave so she could start her exciting new life. We had and have such a sense of ending and sadness at not being part of that new life. I get the same little pangs every time she comes home and leaves again, but it gets easier each time."

Julie Brouhard

"You pack your child off to school and exhale. Then, your child calls, saying somebody she knows is driving your direction and could you please be at a particular place at a particular time to pick her up so she can come home to visit? You are on time and she is late—and God forbid, she would make plans to meet you at a shopping center so you would have something to do while you're waiting! Plus she says she'll be arriving in a red car and, of course, she shows up in a blue car."

Vivian Brown

"So, what if the chosen school turns out to be a mistake for your child? That's okay. The mistake can be erased. Your child can leave at the end of the semester or at the end of the year. Those four years of college are so important. You need to give your child permission to say, 'This is not the right school.'"

Susan Cole

In describing the good-bye process, the word "tension" comes to mind.

The good-bye thing is awash with hopes and dreams, yours and your child's. Most likely, the past year with your youngster has been—um—challenging. So now you think, "Ah, my child is off to college. That means no more tension at home. That means newfound freedom!" Then you realize that your child is gone and nothing will ever be quite the same again.

- Expectations may surface, but be careful. If you create certain expectations for your child, and your child doesn't meet those expectations, where does that leave you? Better stick to less specific hopes and dreams.
- Reality check: When you think about it, you probably don't know as much as you think you do about what's been going on in your child's world for the past 12 to 18 months. Now, you're going to know less. That's why one parent said, "If you don't call me once a week, I'm coming out there for a visit." (The kid called weekly.)
- Before you part, make sure your child understands he can always talk to you. Any time. About anything.
- Your youngster will know when it's time for you to leave. Follow her cues.
- Everyone's thoughts are different at the moment of departure. Most of the time, the daughter wonders how her parents could dare to leave her. The

son wonders how long his parents are going to hang around campus. The mother wonders how long she can draw out the good-byes. The father wonders how long it will take to get back home.

- Don't be surprised if you end up leaving a very homesick child on the campus green. In fact, don't be surprised if that homesickness is still active come Thanksgiving break!
- On the other hand, don't be surprised if your child is devastated when you leave, and then you don't hear from her for weeks because she's so busy getting into this college life thing.

Either way, you've got to give your youngster some space . . . and then let go. (Hard to say. Hard to do.)

Some sage advice: You can't let go if you're hanging on.

Note: E-mail is wonderful!

Especially during that challenging first semester, your child is going to be both on top of the world and in the pits. Again and again and again.

CALLING

Your child will periodically call home to dump all of her problems on you. Then she will hang up and go out to a party. You, on the other hand, will spend the night sitting up in bed, worrying.

No matter what time you call your child during the day, you will no doubt wake him up. This is not necessarily true if you call during the night.

TRANSFER TALK

You may not want to hear this right now, but young people change their minds, just like their parents do. If today's choice becomes tomorrow's mistake, be supportive. "Just gut it out" is probably not a good parental response. "You can transfer" is.

Still, wanting to transfer an hour after freshman orientation concludes isn't recommended. In this case, your student probably can "just gut it out" until the end of the first semester. And maybe even the second semester. Sometimes homesickness lasts longer than the flu.

Kids who transfer from a Big Name University to State U make life tough for their parents because it takes away their bragging rights at cocktail parties!

THE FIRST VISIT HOME

Finally, the child who comes home for that first visit from college will not be the same one you sent away. That's because there are so many outside influences on a college campus. Just remember that all of the lessons you taught in the growing up years are still harbored safely within your child.

Realize, too, this person coming home for a visit is no longer a child but a young adult. That means a major change in your relationship. Your child now knows herself better than you do. Let go and trust. Lovingly.

"When our son was going to preschool for the first time, I was walking him toward the front door when he stopped, looked up at me and said, 'Mom, I can take it from here.' Then he ran into the building. I was locked into that position, crying, when a teacher finally came out, took my hand and said, 'He's okay, Mom.' It was pretty much the same when he went away to college."

Cathy Sweeney

"Do parents cry when they say good-bye to their child? Yes! Our daughter gave us a letter but asked us not to read it until we got back home. The letter said, 'Don't cry.'"

Ben Brouhard

POSTSCRIPT

To give you something to look forward to, we offer three final stories:

"When our daughter came back home, I felt differently. For example, we'd leave her alone, which we absolutely refused to do when she was in high school. I told her there was too much pressure back then, that you never knew who was going to show up. But now, she'd been living on her own for a year. She was more mature. A young adult."

Jane Eckstein

"When our son came home from the Coast Guard Academy that first Christmas, we told him he still had to be in the house by midnight. He couldn't believe it. He said, 'Hey, I'm going to be an officer at the academy!' I said, 'Fine, but in this house, your mother is still the admiral.'"

Rich Kelly

"One night our daughter called home and said, 'Get Mother on the phone. I am only going to say this once.' Your heart just races. Is she in jail? Is she pregnant? Did she get kicked out of school? Finally, her mother picked up another extension and our daughter said, 'Okay, if I spend my junior year abroad, I may not have enough credits to graduate. So I want to know if I can go to school this summer and pick up two classes.' That was it."

Ben Brouhard

SHORT
LIST

THE LONG, MEANDERING
LIST OF COLLEGES

Suggest that your student fill in the following categories for colleges in which he is even somewhat interested. The chart will quickly show a visual comparison of the colleges. Later when it's time to winnow the list for campus visits and possible applications, use The Short, Pretty Serious List of Colleges chart.

College Name	A	B	C	D	E	F	G	H	I	J	K
Accreditation (yes/no)											
Location/Miles from home											
Undergraduate enrollment											
SAT/ACT range											
Faculty-student ratio											
Male-female ratio											
Percent in-state students											
Ethnicity											
Graduation rate (four years)											
Freshman attrition rate											
My possible majors											
Cost											
Housing											
Special services											
Recreation facilities											
On-campus activities											
Greek system											

THE SHORT, PRETTY SERIOUS LIST OF COLLEGES

Suggest that your student fill in the following categories for colleges in which she is strongly considering applying. This chart aims for an in-depth look at the colleges your student has visited or would like to visit. It also starts all of you thinking about the timing of the SAT/ACT tests. Add pertinent categories from The Long, Meandering List of Colleges chart for final comparison, or lay both charts on the dining room table.

College Name	A	B	C	D	E	F	G	H
Friendly students								
Friendly professors, admission representatives								
Visit reactions								
What I remember most								
What I didn't care for								
Dorm rooms								
Dorm overnight								
Computer labs								
Internet access								
Science labs								
Art/music studios								
Size of required courses								
Who teaches freshman courses								
Core curriculum requirements								
Special programs/services								
Internship opportunities								
SAT/ACT requirements								
SAT II requirements								
Application deadline								
Admit notification date								

ROUNDTABLE HOSTS

Roundtables were held in San Diego, California; Miami, Florida; Largo, Maryland; Jefferson City, Missouri; Omaha, Nebraska; Cleveland, Ohio; Clifton, Virginia; Memphis, Tennessee; and Washington, DC.
The hosts were:

Jerry and Laurie Crawford

Cindy Finch

Kathy Hafner

Michael and Raquel Johnston

Diane Lenahan

Susie and Don Polden

Mickey Rudolph

Orlo and Karen Shroyer

Barbara and Dan Walker

Karen Williams

OTHER CONTRIBUTORS

Pam Broome, Educational Consultant, Escaping Failure Paradigm, Springfield, Virginia

Lynn Brown, Counselor, Valley High School, West Des Moines, Iowa

Brenda Easter, Director of Special Programs, Iowa College Student Aid Commission, Des Moines, Iowa

Keith Greiner, Research Director, Iowa College Student Aid Commission, Des Moines, Iowa

Phyllis Grewell, Certified Educational Planner, College Guidance & Planning, West Des Moines, Iowa

M. Kathleen Heikkila, Ed.D., Associate Professor of Education, Graceland College, Lamoni, Iowa

Jane Johnson, Transition Specialist at PACER Center, Minneapolis, Minnesota

Marcy McGahee-Kovac, Special Education Teacher, Fairfax County Public Schools, Virginia

Bob Nordvall, Dean of First Year Students, Gettysburg College, Gettysburg, Pennsylvania

Dennis O'Driscoll, Director of Undergraduate Admissions at Creighton University, Omaha, Nebraska

Anne Marie Pflanz, The Travel Center, Des Moines, Iowa

Donna Wilkin, Ph.D., Assistant Superintendent of Teaching & Learning, West Des Moines Community Schools, West Des Moines, Iowa

Barb Zurek, Teacher, Houston, Texas

ROUNDTABLE PARTICIPANTS

Jim Adams
Sheila Ayala
Joyce Batipps
Cathy Belter
Bud Bennett
Cyndi Bennett
Pamela Broome
Ben H. Brouhard
Julie Brouhard
Vivian Brown
Susan Cole
Jerry Crawford
Laurie Crawford
Jim Dakin
Karen Dakin
Paula Dawson
Liz DeMik
Henry C. Doll
Mary Doll

Gene Eckstein
Jane Eckstein
Susie Edwards
Jacquie Evans
Jim Evans
Cindy Finch
Ann Galles
Lee Galles
Elaine Gingerich
Wally Gingerich
David Hafner
Deborah Hafner
Kathy Hafner
Claudia Harkins
Eunice Harris
Diane Hayes
Janet Heimbuch
Ken Heimbuch
Jeanie Heskett
John Heskett

Nancy Johnson
John Johnson
Michael Johnston
Raquel Johnston
Nancy Jones
Rich Kelly
Rose Kelly
Joe Kirsch
Ronni Kirsch
Daniel Lazzaro
Mary Beth Lazzaro
Diane Lenahan
Dr. Michael A. Merlin
Jennifer Merlin
Diana Pace
Peter Pashler
Rickie Pashler

Dianne Peterson
Don Polden
Susie Polden
Joyce Pope
Jerry Rewa
Dennis Rhodes
Mickey Rudolph
Karen Shroyer
Orlo Shroyer
Cathy Sweeney
Chris Sweeney
Audrey Valhuerdi
Barbara Walker
Dan Walker
Gail Walzer
Jay Welch
Marge Welch
Maricel York

RESOURCES

WEB SITES:

Project EASI Access for Students and Institutions *http://easi.ed.gov/*—Post-high school education planning and funding.

College Bound *http://minot.com/~nansen/college.html*—Scholarships, financial aid, testing, and colleges.

Embark.com *www.embark.com/*—Test preparation, career exploration, financial aid, finding colleges, shopping, message boards, and electronic applications.

CollegeLink *www.collegelink.com*—College, financial aid, and scholarship applications.

Fast WEB *www.studentservices.com/fastweb/*—Scholarship searches, a college directory, and information on topics from admissions to jobs after college.

FinAid, the Financial Aid Information Page *www.finaid.org/*—Comprehensive, objective information about student financial aid including loans, scholarships, military aid, how to apply and fill out the forms, and a calculator to figure the Expected Family Contribution.

Review.com at *www.review.com*—by The Princeton Review, on-line research, selection, and application tools, and discussion groups for parents and kids.

Barron's Educational Series, Inc. *www.barronseduc.com/*—Database of Barron's publications on college planning, guides, and test preparation as well as purchase information.

Independent Educational Consultants Association (IECA), web site at *www.educationalconsulting.org*—3251 Old Lee Highway, Suite 510, Fairfax, VA 22030; 703-591-4850; E-mail: *iecaassoc@aol.com*

LDOnLine *www.ldonline.com/*—Guide to learning disabilities for parents, children, and teachers, including resources and a bulletin board.

National Information Center for Children and Youth with Disabilities *www.nichcy.org*—Information and referral center for disabilities and disability-related issues. P.O. Box 1492, Washington, DC 20013; 1-800-695-0285 (Voice/TT) and (202) 884-8200 (Voice/TT).

BOOKS:

Antonoff, Steven. *The College Finder: Choosing the School That's Right for You, rev. ed.* New York: Fawcett Book Group, 1999. Profiles colleges targeting everything from the academic to the social.

Bissinger, H. G. *Friday Night Lights*. Reading, Massachusetts: Addison-Wesley Publishing Co., 1990. High school football players' dreams and quest for fame and college.

Boyer, Ernest L. and Paul Boyer. *Smart Parents' Guide to College*. Princeton, New Jersey: Peterson's Guides, 1996. Ten important factors for students and parents to consider in the college selection process.

Burnham, Amy, Daniel Kaufman and Chris Dowhan. *Essays That Will Get You into College*. Hauppauge, New York: Barron's Educational Series,

Inc., 1998. Examples of essays by admitted students, what admissions officers look for, and the how-to process.

Coburn, Karen Levin and Madge Lawrence Treeger. *Letting Go: A Parent's Guide to Understanding the College Years, 3rd ed.* New York: Harper Perennial, 1997. Helps parents learn to let their college children leave the nest.

Editors of Barron's Educational Series, Inc. *Profiles of American Colleges w/Software, 23rd ed.* Hauppauge, New York, 1998. Lists more than 1,600 accredited U.S. colleges with complete objective information including location, number of students and faculty, test score range, graduation rate, and programs. Visit the Barron's website at *www.barronseduc.com*

Lamm, Kathryn. *10,000 Ideas for Term Papers, Projects and Reports.* New York: Simon & Schuster, 1991. Possible topics for essays.

McGinty, Sarah Myers. *The College Application Essay.* New York: The College Board, 1997. A how-to book using the student's unique strengths to match up with what admissions officers seek.

Worthington, Janet Farrar and Ronald Farrar. *The Ultimate College Survival Guide: Proven Tips and Techniques for Success.* Princeton, New Jersey: Peterson's Guides, 1998.

INDEX